Nos Ancêtres

1

BIOGRAPHIES D'ANCÊTRES

AUDET — BÉRUBÉ — BLAIS — BLANCHET —
COUTURE — DEBLOIS — DIONNE — FORTIN —
GAGNON — LACASSE — LAVERGNE — LEROY —
LESSARD — LÉVESQUE — PAQUIN — PARADIS —
PILOTE — POTHIER — RHÉAUME — RONDEAU —
SAVARD — TRUDEAU — VACHON — VEILLEUX.

2e édition
ISBN-2-89238-052-9

Sainte-Anne-de-Beaupré 1981

A Review

From the "MEMOIRES de la Societe Genealogique Canadienne-Francaise," No. 143, Volume XXXI No. 1 Jan.-Fev.-Mars 1980. Page 69.

By Father Gerard Lebel C.Ss.R., *Nos Ancetres*. Ancestral biographies of the oldest of the French-Canadian families. **Edition: Saint-Anne-de-Beaupre, 1980.** Twenty-four biographies, 145 pages in all.

"The author is an expert on original documentation. He has searched the archives and knows the best sources. Many of the ancestral biographies that he presents are little known, others more so. However, in this sort of research, facts often suffer in the telling and become swallowed up by legend and folklore. Not so with Father Lebel. He sticks to the historical truth when combing his sources. Even the professional genealogists will have a great deal to learn from this welcome little book."

R.P. Julien Deziel, President
Societe Genealogique Canadienne-Francaise

OUR FRENCH-CANADIAN ANCESTORS

By

Thomas J. Laforest

FIRST EDITION

**PALM HARBOR, FLORIDA
1983**

ALL RIGHTS RESERVED

LIBRARY OF CONGRESS CATALOG CARD NUMBER
83-081941

ISBN 0-914163-01-9 (Volume 1)
ISBN 0-914163-00-0 (Series)

Printed in the United States of America

Published and distributed by The LISI Press,
a subsidiary of Laforest International Service Inc.
P.O. Box 1063, Palm Harbor, Florida 33563

Price $10.50 plus $1.50
for postage and handling

Dedication

To My Father

THOMAS ADOLPHE LAFOREST
1889-1980

a seventh generation
French - Canadian - American

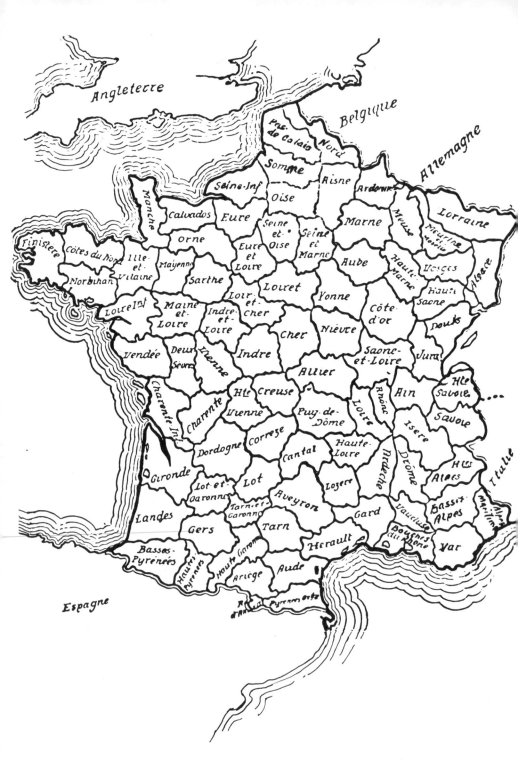

DEPARTEMENTS DE FRANCE

iv

Table of Contents

Table of Contents
(Continued)

Table of Contents
(Concluded)

APPENDICES

"A defaut de savoir ou l'on va,
on peut savoir d'ou l'on vient!

The End

Acknowledgements

The author and publisher would like to thank all those who gave of their time, effort and permission to help make this little book a reality.

Among others, we are grateful to:

J. Raymond Beaulieu, Director, Corporate Communications, La Brasserie Labatt Limitee for the use of the portraits of Our Ancestors, taken from *Les Anciennes Familles du Quebec.*

Professor Marcel Trudel, Doctor of Letters, University of Ottawa, author of *An Atlas of New France,* and Marc Boucher, Directeur Interimaire, Les Presses de L'Universite Laval, for the use of notes and maps from the *Atlas.*

Father Gerard Lebel, C.Ss.R., for his notes, references and sources, on which a bibliography from *Nos Ancetres* was compiled.

Professor James M.S. Careless, University of Toronto, author of *Canada: A Story of Challenge,* and Moira Jones, Permissons Editor of Gage Publishing Company, for permission to reprint from the above title.

Curator Raymond Gariepy, Canadian National Archives; and La Societe Historique de Quebec, for use of maps from *Cahiers d'Histoire No. 27,* A publication of the Society authored by him.

James and Ruth Weathers, Weathers Graphic Design, for the artwork, typography, proofreading and original presentation of the portraits of nine of Our Ancestors not heretofor seen in print.

James Hargett, Executive Vice-president of Interprint Incorporated, Clearwater, Florida, for his personal supervision of the typesetting and printing of this book.

THE PROVINCES OF FRANCE
UNDER THE OLD REGIME

Foreword

This English version of NOS ANCETRES, retitled OUR FRENCH-CANADIAN ANCESTORS, is the first of a series intended for those descendants who have migrated far afield, but especially for those who may be no longer conversant in French.

When the author asked me to make the bridge between our cultures, he knew that I had a foot in each one. Like all of you I am proud of my heritage and I carry my name with honor. Also like most of you, I do not speak French, even though I do read it and hope you enjoy this translation.

Speaking of translation, I have purposely not tampered with the names of people or places. As a professional geographer, I know that one map is worth a thousand words, therefore you will find many in this book. Additionally, in the belief that most of our readers will not be genealogists, beyond an historical interest in family, I have included a Glossary of French words and phrases found in the sources referred to in the Bibliography.

The vignettes, from THE LIFE OF NEW FRANCE 1663 - 1760, are an addition, not found in the original, and especially slanted for the American reader. The chapters concerning Our Ancestors and the King's Daughters are the same as first written, with updating of course.

For dedicated genealogists, I have added a Bibliography, an Index of Names, and the annotation necessary to open the door to further research.

For those of you who would like to keep a record of your own ancestors, or even of today's family, I have included a Family Record Sheet. Before marking up the original in the book, simply flatten out the back cover, lay the book face up on a copy machine and run off as many as you need, and a few for your relatives as well.

In summation, I would be pleased to receive your comments, constructive criticism and/or suggestions for improvements for inclusion in Volume 2.

Thomas J. Laforest
Professor of Geography
P.O. Box 1063
Palm Harbor, FL 33563

Introduction

By The Author

Our history is a heritage. Those men who came from the old world brought with them a civilization whose roots were buried deep in the Middle Ages. The France of King Francis I, of Louis XIII, and of Louis XIV, established a New France in the Saint Lawrence River Valley. There France sent those men and women who were the better part of her heart: Champlain and Maisonneuve, Marguerite Bourgeoys and Jeanne Mance, Talon and Frontenac, the Recollects and the Jesuits, the Ursulines and the Hospitalliers, not to forget Monseigneur Francois de Laval, Bishop of Quebec. These figureheads of our glorious past inspired us and gave direction to our present lives. They led the way and we followed.

Each era reaffirms old truths in new forms. The brighter the flame burns at the foot of the cenotaph and at the monuments to the Unknown Soldier, the brighter is the memory of those thousands of ordinary people who gave their lives to establish a homeland. For all too long they remained buried in dusty archives and forgotten between the yellowed pages of parish registers. As a result, oral tradition often exaggerated facts in the recounting of legends. After the turn of the last century—especially after publication of the colossal work of Monseigneur Cyprian Tanguay—historians and genealogists set themselves to the task of writing the history of the early French-Canadian families by researching their origins.

Within the limited scope of this book, we have set out to give our genealogical contribution by polishing the many facets of those jewels who became the founders of our families. The twenty-four forefathers of the families comprising this First Volume were, for the most part, very humble craftsmen. Their stories have already appeared in the **Saint Anne Review** in French, but for this English edition, we have augmented, corrected and brought them up to date.

Our objective has been not to tell all there is to tell, an impossible task, but to arouse your interest and curiosity. Given this start, you the reader may search, find and be rewarded by additional knowledge of your own French-Canadian heritage.

I thank my two collaborators, the Reverend Fathers Gabriel U. Gagnon and M. Renald Lessard, who, through filial respect, have seen fit to present the story of their own ancestors.

Gerard Lebel, C.Ss.R.
Ste. Anne-de-Beaupre
P.Q. Canada GOA 3CO

Bourgeois Canadienne 17th Century

Chapter 1

Life in New France, 1663 - 1760

THE STRUCTURE OF SOCIETY

*I*n the time of New France, and particularly after 1663 when the colony began to thrive, a distinctive way of life worked out in Canada. It still leaves its mark on French Canada today. A glance at the society of New France not only reveals the world of the seventeenth-century colonists but throws light on the life and outlook of the modern French Canadians, who form nearly one-third of the present Canadian population.

To begin with , life in New France was fashioned on authoritarian lines: that is, power was concentrated at the top of society, and the mass of the colonists were used to obeying authority, not to governing their own lives. This did not necessarily mean an attitude of dependence or meek docility. The people of New France showed their sturdy self-reliance in other ways. Yet in matters of religion, government, and relations between classes of people, French Canada readily accepted direction from above. There was little of the demand for religious independence and self-government, or the levelling of social distinctions which generally marked the English colonies to the south. In these unruly provinces the trend was toward democracy and the emphasis was on liberty. New France instead put its faith in ordered authority, not disorderly freedom, and stressed duties, not rights.

The forms of government helped shape this attitude in New France. All power depended finally on the King. He and his ministers at Versailles supervised even the minor details of government in the colony, and little could be done without their direction. Their control might have been well-intentioned, kindly, or even wise; but it was absolute. This was paternal absolutism at its best and worst. It developed in New France the habit of looking beyond herself for guidance and leadership. Similarly, the government within New France was absolute and paternal as far as the inhabitants were concerned. Except for the popularly chosen captains of militia in each parish, there were no agencies of local self-government, nor elected bodies voicing public opinion. A few attempts to include elected representatives in the councils of government were soon cut short. New France never learned to manage its own affairs—or even to ask to do so.

The society of French Canada was also hierarchical in structure: it was graded into distinctly separate upper and lower layers. The bulk of the colonists, or habitants, were farmers and formed the broad lower order. On the upper levels were the government officials, the large landholders, or seigneurs, and the principal clergy. In between the two main groups the wealthy fur-trade merchants and the ordinary fur traders did, in a sense, represent a commercial or middle class. In reality, however, New France had virtually no middle class. The big fur merchants tended to be closely linked with the government officials; and since there was little commerce in the colony apart from the fur trade, and no industry to speak of, there were very few tradesmen and only a handful of artisans. They did not form an effective middle class.

As for the ordinary fur trader, he hardly belonged to the colony at all. His world lay far beyond in the forest. He visited the settled areas only occasionally to obtain his earnings, spent his money on a wild spree, and disappeared again into the woods. The life of the independent fur trader, the *coureur-de-bois,* seemed glamorous and free (actually it might be bitterly hard) and it attracted many reckless spirits away from the farmlands. But, far from the fur trader forming a real part of the society of the colony, he almost represented a minus quantity, a subtraction from it.

Accordingly, with hardly any middle class between upper and lower orders in French Canada, the division in society was clear-cut, indeed. Furthermore, the system of land-holding established definite social distinctions. Land was held according to the seigneurial system. It was granted in large blocks to the seigneurs, who rented it in smaller holdings to the habitant farmers. The habitants paid their seigneur various forms of rent and performed certain services for him. The result was to create two groups on the land: the seigneurs, who were landlords with special privileges and authority, and the habitants, tenant farmers, who owed not only rent and services but honor and respect as well. In the English colonies, on the other hand, while there might be large and small farmers, and sometimes landlords and tenants, there were not the same class divisions fixed by law, and most farmers owned their own land. (1)

The seigneurial system, therefore, was a major factor in making the society of New France authoritarian and hierarchical in character. It entered widely into the life of the colony, and so deserves more investigation. This will be presented in Volume 2 of the series.

Bibliography

(1)   N. Pages 59 - 61
Reprinted with the permission of the author, J.M.S. Careless, and the publisher, Macmillan of Canada, a Division of Gage Publications, Limited.

DAUGHTERS OF THE KING

Les Filles Du Roi

Chapter 2

The King's Daughters

$\mathscr{B}$efore 1660, the first girls who came to Canada looking for a husband were known as "filles des marier," or marriageable daughters. They were few in number and often made their own way, paying for the passage by a contract of indenture. After 1663 the French royal authorities became concerned with the peopling of the colony. The King himself directed the recruitment of young women of good quality for this purpose. Hence the appellation, Les Filles du Roi or Daughters of the King, called by many, "The King's Girls."

In the early days the recruitment concentrated on "demoiselles;" girls with a good background and even a litle education, suited for the military officers and men of property. Also the initial recruitments were mostly city girls from Paris and surrounding suburbs. This did not work out too well. The King's man in the colony, Intendant Jean Talon, was obviously responding to the demands of the habitants, when he asked Minister Colbert to send out "strong, intelligent and beautiful girls of robust health, habituated to farm work." Indeed, the bachelors wanted strong partners who could do their share of the work. A not uncommon sight in those days before draft animals had been bred in sufficient numbers, was that of the wife pulling the plow and her husband pushing with one hand, while holding a musket at the ready in the other. It is no coincidence then that most of the girls came from the farm country of Normandy and the Ile-de-France. (1)

Having been selected by recommendation from her parish priest, the girl was promised a dowry by the King. It came to 50 livres if she married a soldier or habitant, or 100 livres if she married an officer. But what did the girl receive before leaving France? The one thing all the girls had in common was poverty, hence a real need to be outfitted. The author is indebted to Raymond Douville and to J.D. Casanova, who wrote *La Vie Quotidienne en Nouvelle France,* in 1964, noting these details:

"To this statutory grant (the dowry cited above) other essential expenses were added. The first disbursement was set at 100 livres: 10 for personal and moving expenses, 30 for clothing and 60 for the passage. In addition to the aforesaid clothing, the following: a small hope chest, 1 head dress, 1 taffeta handkerchief, 1 pair of shoe ribbons, 100 sewing needles, 1 comb, 1 spool of white thread, 1 pair of stockings, 1 pair of gloves, 1 pair of scissors, 2 knives, 1,000 pins, 1 bonnet, 4 lace braids and 2 livres in silver money. On arrival the Sovereign Council of New France provided the girls with some clothing suitable to the climate and some provisions drawn from the Kings warehouse."

The men eagerly awaited the arrival of the girls and the selection process was a hurry up affair. Nevertheless, the girl could pick and choose, often to the point of exercising her prerogative a few times over. When the match had been made, the newly married couple was given 50 livres to buy provisions, plus an ox and a cow, 2 pigs, a pair of chickens, 2 barrels of salt meat and 11 crowns in money. This was supposed to give the newlyweds a start. (2)

Thus provided for, some 852 of these King's Daughters arrived in New France during the ten year period from 1663 to 1673. These ladies comprised about 17% of the total population of New France, estimated at less than 5000 souls during this same time. The bracing climate of Canada was said to be particularly advantageous to women. Dollier de Casbon wrote from Montreal, "Though the cold is very wholesome to both sexes, it is incomparably more so to the female, who is almost immortal here." (2)

Even though many Frenchmen married Indian girls, the squaws did not have many children; but not so the King's Daughters! The Intendant Talon reported that in 1670 most of the girls who had arrived in 1669 were already pregnant and that in 1671 nearly 700 children were borne by them. Without exaggeration it can be said that these women created a nation, from which millions of us have peopled both Canada and the United States.

The province of origin of these 852 daughters of the king are as follows: (3)

Ile-de-France	314	Brie	5
Normandie	153	Berry	5
Aunis	86	Auvergne	5
Champagne	43	Limousin	4
Poitou	38	Angoumois	3
Anjou	22	Provence	3
Beauce	22	Savoie	3
Maine	19	Franche-Comte'	2
Orleanais	19	Gascogne	2

BIBLIOGRAPHY

(1)   R.   Pages 282 - 286
(2)   Y.   From the tables.
(3)   S.   Additionally, this reference contains a complete list of the 852 Kings Daughters by name and marriage.

Nicolas Audet

Chapter 3

Nicolas Audet
dit
Lapointe

$\mathcal{N}$icolas Audet, born about 1641, was the son of Innocent Audet and Vincente Riene (Roy), of Saint-Pierre-Maille, in the Diocese of Poitiers. We know that he came to Canada before 1664 because there is a record of his confirmation at Quebec on 23 March of that year.(1)

Poitiers is a town in Poitou; that beautiful and bountiful province of France where wheat is grown, the vine is cultivated and many varieties of fruit are raised. It is wooded country, yet covered by excellent pastureland; in this province Charles Martel repulsed the Saracins and Clovis battled the Goths.

Just about all of the colonists who came from France in the 17th century started in one of three ways: by working for the government, by working for a religious order, or by working for one of the more prosperous landowners. Nicolas seems to have been taken under the wing of Monseigneur Francois de Laval, Bishop of Quebec. In the census of 1666 we find him working on the farm owned by the Bishop, at Saint-Joachim nearby Cape Tourmente. (2) Two years later, he was still working for the Bishop as a porter in the lordly Chateau of Quebec. Confirmation of this comes through an act of the Notary Pierre Duquet, (3) dated 13 October 1668, which records: "Today, at the entrance gate of the estate, Sieur Jean Madry rang a little bell, in response to which he was met by Nicolas Audet, porter of the Chateau. After admitting him, Audet went to inform his master, the Bishop."

For more than four years Nicolas worked in service for others, earning his way. In preparing for his future he was counting more on savings than on credit.

THE SETTLER

Nicolas Audet, the porter, decided to become a settler on the Ile d'Orleans, just opposite the Beaupre coast. On 22 June 1667, he received a concession from his Bishop, "of three arpents of land fronting on the Saint Lawrence River and running southward . . ." His grant was in the parish of Sainte-Famille, from which the parish of Saint-Jean was later formed. His neighbors were Guy Boivin and Robert Boulay. He hired them "to help him build a house to be finished within one year from this day."

Each year, on the Feast of Saint Martin, the 11th of November, he was required to give 20 sols in seigneurial rent for each arpent of river frontage, 12 deniers for "cens" and 3 capons chosen by the Seigneur. It is worth noting that the signatures on the contract for the land, other than that of the Notary Paul Vachon, are those of: Jean Crete, Master Cartwright; of Paul de Rainville, Sheriff of Beauport and, of the Bishop of Quebec himself. Nicolas Audet appears to have been well connected! (4)

As soon as he could, Nicolas busied himself building his house with the help of his neighbors. The census of 1681 tells us that by then he had cleared 15 arpents of land and had acquired 6 animals. (5)

A KING OF THE HEARTH

Having built a house, Nicolas sought to make it a home. To this end, he courted Magdeleine Despres, a young girl of fourteen years. These two betrothed appeared before the Notary Romain Becquet at Quebec, 30 August 1670, to arrange a contract of marriage. (6) The future bride was sponsored by "Dame Anne Gagnier, widow of the late Master Jean Bourdon and by Madamoiselle Elizabeth Etienne." In accordance with the custom of the time,

11

Magdeleine would bring Nicolas a dowry, a considerable one it seems. She had saved or acquired 200 livres, but also she would receive "the sum of 50 livres given her by His Majesty, in consideration of her marriage." In short, these two were hardly poor in material goods. This help given Magdeleine by the King signifies that she was alone in Canada, most likely an orphan. We know that she could write; she penned herself as the daughter of Francois Despres and of Magdeleine Le Grand from the Parish of Saint-Sauveur in Paris. This young lady, born about 1656, was one of many generous girls who came to Canada under the protection of the King of France.

At Sainte-Famille the following September 15th, the missionary priest Father Thomas Morel, blessed their union in the presence of the witnesses Pierre Rondeau and Mathurin Dube. When Pierre and Mathurin were married the year before, each in turn had asked Nicolas to stand up for him, now the favor was being returned. (7)

This marriage brought forth twelve children: 9 boys and 3 girls, but the elder two died young. All were born in the Parish of Sainte-Famille except the youngest three who were born at Saint-Jean. These ten children founded the family line: they were all married on the Island except Marguerite. She married Louis-Emery Coderre at Boucherville on 26 August 1722. It is believed that she followed her brother Joachim there, after the death of her parents, when he married Louise Roberge. (8)

In 1689 old Nicolas fell gravely ill, a situation from which he never fully recovered. He was hospitalized for 19 consecutive days in the heat of the August summer and in September he spent 26 more days under the care of the nursing sisters at the Hotel-Dieu in Quebec. Heretofore he had always worked his farm with a stubborn tenacity, but no more would he be active.

He had seen to the marriage of three of his children: Nicolas, Pierre and Madeleine, but that still left seven children at home, to be cared for by the strong arms of his wife alone. But he could still plan ahead and, on 9 July 1696, he acquired yet another concession. This grant of land was of 3 arpents in river frontage some distance to the west of his own place. On 2 August 1698, he gave this land to his son Jean-Baptiste. (9)

There were so many things yet to be done, but the bell tolled for Nicolas when he was 59 years old. He was buried on 10 December 1700 in the cemetery at Sain-Jean, where his headstone bore the surname Lapointe. His widow passed on her inheritance by donation to her son Joseph on 1 October 1703. (10) An inventory of the belongings of old Nicolas was made by Notary Etienne Jacob on 27 September 1706. It recorded 75 arpents of usable land, a nearly new house measuring 18 × 24 feet, a shed and a stable. (11)

Magdeleine Despres survived her husband for twelve years and at her death children Joachim and Madeleine were still unmarried. She was buried beside him, on 19 December 1712, at the age of 56. (12)

POSTHUMOUS GLORIES

The Audet's truly could be called a religious family. For 150 years they gave hundreds of priests and other religious, to the Roman Catholic Church of Canada. One example is that of His Excellency Monseigneur Lionel Audet, son of Louis Audet, cartwright, and Eugenie Turcotte. The Monseigneur was born at Saint-Marie de Beauce, laureated a Doctor of Theology, then consecrated a Bishop on 1 May 1952. He is still the Auxilliary Bishop of Quebec a quarter-century later.

The first French-Canadian to be appointed to the Court of the Exchequer was the Honorable Judge Arthur Audette.

As of 4 April 1972, he was the youngest Judge so appointed.

The legendary Alexis "Le Trotteur," was born on 4 June 1860 at La Malbaie. His parents were Francois Audet dit Lapointe and Delphine Tremblay. He, too, was a descendant of the Old Ancestor Nicolas Audet. (13)

The following variations of the family name have sprung from descendants of Our Ancestor: Audette, Bailleul de Pierre-Cot, Hode, Lapointe, Odet and Simon. (14)

BIBLIOGRAPHY

(1)	BU	No. 57, page 1141
(2)	CX	Vol. IV, page 54, col. b
(3)	CB & Z	13 October 1668
(4)	CB & DK	22 June 1667
(5)	CR & CD	18 April 1682
(6)	CB & K	30 August 1670 and 2 October 1673
(7)	G	Privately printed family history
(8)	DH	Privately printed family history, page 158
(9)	CB & AH	2 August 1698 and 10 March 1704
(10)	CB & AS	1 October 1703
(11)	CB & AS	7 September 1706
(12)	AK	Vol. 1 pages 449 - 554
	CE	Vol. 32 - 32 pages 532 - 533
(13)	BM	Vol. 12 pages 99 - 100
(14)	CZ	Vol. 7 page 496

Damien Bérubé

Chapter 4

Damien Berube

*W*ho does not know the words of the song: "Will I ever again see my Normandy?" It is because we all have Norman blood in our veins. More than 1300 men and women from Normandy crossed the Atlantic in order to conquer Canada, not to mention the 43 Jesuits of whom 4 earned the halo of sainthood and martyrdom.

Damien Berube came from Normandy. His ancestors had their roots among the Scandinavian adventurers under Rolland the Conquerer, who in 911, subjugated parts of Normandy: Talou, the regions of Caux and of Roumois. (1)

Damien Berube came from the town of Rocquefort, a suburb of Fauville-en-Caux. Arrondissement of Yvetot, Department of Seine-Maritime. His baptismal certificate, dated 2 February 1647, reads "Damien Berrube son of Robert and of Catherine Ferrocog." His godfather was Jean-Baptiste Deschamps, Sieur of Boishebert, Seigneur of Costecoste, of Montaubert, and of Landres; father of the future Seigneur of Riviere-Ouelle. As for the godmother, she was named Catherine Henry (?), and was not married to the godfather, whose wife was Elizabeth Debin. (2)

OCCUPATION STONEMASON

Jean-Baptiste Deschamps, Sieur de la Bouteillerie, had obtained permission from the Sun King to go out and clear the land between Trois-Rivieres and Montreal up to the limit of a thousand arpents. The SAINT-JEAN-BAPTISTE, a ship of 300 tons, departed toward the end of July 1671.

She carried on board a cargo of about 100 men, of whom two were masons; Damien Berube and Jacques Miville dit Deschenes, and two were carpenters; Robert Leveque and J. Thomas Thiboutot. The supercargo consisted of 26 women from Paris, 10 mules, 50 sheep and several items useful for trading. The Seigneur Deschamps, because of the Iroquois menace, did not take up his original land grant. Instead he directed his efforts toward Riviere-Ouelle, there to take up a new concession obtained on 29 October 1672, from the King's representative Jean Talon. (3)

Initially Damien helped his seigneur build a manor house on the land where today the parish church stands. Then, in 1679, he built a little mill on a nearby brook. It was the first windmill, the EVENTAIL, in New France. The seigneur then had him build five more in different spots on the estate.

On 27 September 1676, Damien received a significant concession of his own, "12 arpents fronting on the river Ouelle, to a depth of 40 arpents, bordered on one side by the land taken back from Thiboutot, and on the other by that part of the land not granted in 1672." In spite of all the work he was doing on building stone walls, Damien still found time to clear 10 arpents of land and get it under cultivation. According to the census of 1681, he also had 6 head of cattle and one good gun for self defense, but more often used to hunt those marvellous game birds and animals that abounded in the vicinity. (5)

In 1684, de la Bouteillerie gave a piece of land for the construction of a humble chapel. Jacques Miville and Damien Berube did the work on the stone foundations. Father Thomas Morel blessed this modest temple, dedicated to Our-Lady-of-Liesse, on her Feast Day in the year 1685. (6)

17

FATHER OF A FAMILY

After eight years of looking around the countryside, Damien finally found himself a companion to suit his taste. Her name was Jeanne Sauvenier (Savonet or Latour dit Simonet). This orphan, born in Paris in 1646, was the daughter of Jacques and Antoinette Babilotte, widow of Jean Soucy dit Lavigne, and inhabitant of the Ile-aux-Oies and mother of four children by Soucy: Anne, Pierre, Marie-Anne and Guillaume. When one truly loves it seems one does not lack courage, even to wedding a 32-year-old woman with 4 children. The marriage was blessed on the Island on 22 August 1679 by the missionary priest Morel. Assisting at the ceremony were Father Paul Dupuy, Squire Noel Langlois, who was also Seigneur of the Ile-aux-Oies, Guillaume Lemieux and Jean Peltier.

The Berube couple brought 7 children into the world, of whom 3 died at an early age. Pierre, Ignace and Mathurin married into the families Dancause, Ouellet and Miville respectively. Jeanne-Marguerite married Rene Plourde on 26 August 1697.

PREMATURE DEPARTURE

Our Ancestor Berube was laid low by an illness during the prime of life. His head full of grand dreams, his home full of beautiful children; to them he made his goodbyes and left for Heaven at the age of 41. He was buried at Riviere-Ouelle on 7 March 1688. In the space of just a few years he had cleared 20 arpents of land on his vast domain, provided for the 4 children of his wife, fathered 7 offspring of his own, but did not live to see his baby son Mathurin, who was born after his death. He opened the way for the Berube line of descendents, both numerous and respectable. He is the progenitor of all the Berube's both in Canada and the United States.

The cause of the death of Our Ancestor calls for a word of explanation. Paul-Henri Hudon, author of a parish monograph of Riviere Ouelle, puts his finger on it: "There was in that year (1688) in New France some epidemics of influenza, of measles and of all sorts of fevers." The following day, 8 March, the two little Berube girls, 2-year-old Therese and 5-year-old Marie, were both buried at the same place as their father.

THE KING'S FAVORITE

The mother house of the Misericorde, founded at Paris in 1624 by President Seguier, was destined to receive 100 orphans—those without either a father or a mother. These girls, educated according to the principles of the Catholic religion, were schooled in arts and letters as well. From time to time they were called upon to put on recitations and plays at Court. Was Jeanne Sauvenier one of those protected by the King? No doubt about it since she was educated and proved her abililty to read and write before a notary. (7) One must point out the clever arrangements she made in the agreement to provide for the 4 children of her first husband, as well as those of her second. In 1689, her daughter Anne Soucy married Jean Lebel. Then for a third time, Jeanne married on 7 November 1692 at Riviere-Ouelle, to Francois Miville. He was the widower of Marie Langlois, father of five children, of whom Joseph, Jacques and Charles were minors still under their father's care. In order to add to this menage, Jeanne had one last child to give to Miville: Marie-Francoise, baptised in 1694, later married to Prisque Boucher, and mother of fourteen children. So we see that Jeanne Sauvenier had 12 children in all: 4 by Soucy, 7 by Berube and 1 by Miville.

Her contract with Francois Miville stipulated "to hold no property in common between them, notwithstanding custom and usage . . . ." Jeanne set about to inventory her belongings with the help of Guillaume Lizotte and Rene Ouelette, in the presence of Robert Leveque. Then it came time to carry out the provisions for inheritance fairly and judiciously. Oft times such occasions are made for quarreling and bickering, but nothing of the sort took place. Jeanne signed a donation before the Cure Bernard de Roqueleyne, sent by the Intendent for this purpose. By this act, she gave the inheritance from Damien Berube back to his children in 4 equal parts. As for the livestock, they were divided in two lots, one for the Berube children, the other for the Soucys. Then the last child, Francoise, whose father was still living, renounced her part of the inheritance in favor of her half brothers and sisters. Jeanne and her husband retained the right of occupancy during their lifetime. Pierre Berube, who inherited the piece of property with the house on it, accepted the guardianship of his mother and her husband, Francois Miville. This act was recorded by the notary Janneau on 15 November 1708. (8)

PERSONAL AND REAL ESTATE

The land, 12×24 arpents, contained an old house, a shed, an old stable, a pigsty, 5 head of cattle, 3 horses, 7 pigs, 7 sheep, 12 chickens, a rooster and 2 turkeys. The inventory listed more than five dozen articles of personal effects, some of which had belonged to Jean Soucy. The debts to be paid off came to more than 437 livres.

A LIFETIME LEASE

In return for the early assignment of their inheritance, the children were required to furnish the parents each year: 2 bushels of wheat, 10 pounds of good and salable lard, etc. She and her husband could even make maple sugar in the springtime for their personal use. This lifetime lease was to continue for one year after the death of Jeanne in order to pay for her funeral and to have 25 Masses celebrated for the repose of her soul.

UNTO THEIR GLORY

Jeanne Sauvenier passed on in 1721 at the age of about 74 years. Her funeral took place at Riviere-Ouelle on the 21st of March, 10 years after the death of her third husband, Francois Miville.

Among her descendants, Octave Soucy was born at Saint Andre de Kamouraska on 13 March 1841, son of

Benjamin and Marie Genevieve Paradis. A sixth-generational Canadian, he was the first priest to bear the name of Soucy. Jean-Francois, born at Trois-Pistoles on 27 July 1827, also of the sixth generation, the son of Felix and of Thecle Cote, became the first Berube priest in 1855.

It would be appropriate here to pay particular attention to the life of this not-so-ordinary wife. This occasion is a good time to highlight the irreplaceable work of these strong women who played such a large part in the foundation of our country. Let us give honor to Our Ancestors and honor to their wives!

BIBLIOGRAPHY

(1)	BI	page 182
(2)	BM	Bersyl, La Famille Berube, Vol. XVIII, pages 159 - 168
(3)	V	Vol. II, pages 188 - 189
(4)	AP	page 462 et passim
(5)	CB & AH	31 October 1692
(6)	BF	Vol. 52, pages 143 - 145
(7)	Y	pages 332 - 333
(8)	CB & AT	4 October 1712

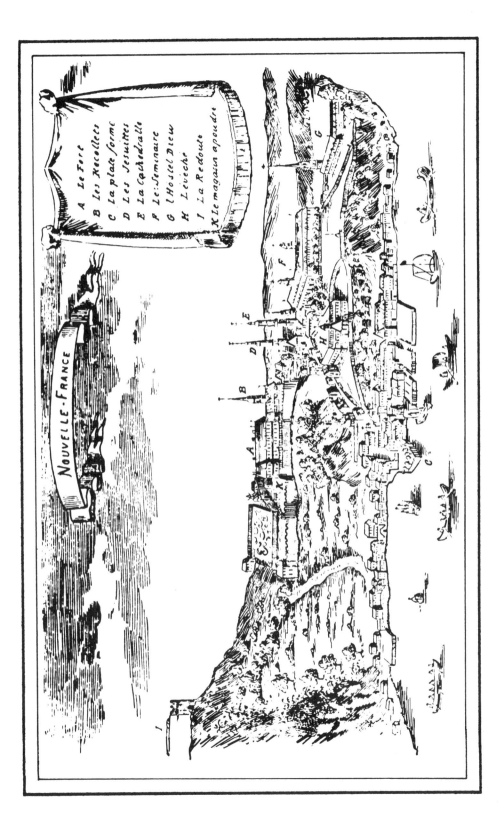

NOUVELLE-FRANCE

A Le Fort
B Les Recollets
C La place forme
D Les Jesuittes
E La Cathedralle
F Le Seminaire
G l'Hospel Dieu
H L'evêche
I La Redoute
K Le magasin a poudre

Pierre Blais

Chapter 5

Pierre Blais

*I*n France, the family name Blais has many variations: Ble, Blay, Bled, Belet and Blet. Blais is the most popular form of the original Blaise, a physician who lived at Sebastia in Armenia, became a Bishop and was martyred in the year 316. The wool-carding guild chose him as patron saint because his executioners cut him to ribbons with iron combs before beheading him. It is this Saint Blaise whose protection is still invoked against sore throats.

But let us discuss Our Ancestor Pierre Blais, colonist on the Ile d'Orleans in the Saint Lawrence River.

DEPARTURE

Pierre Blet probably left France from the port of La Rochelle in the Province of Aunis in 1664; destination Canada. The Dutch ship NOIR, under the command of Captain Pierre Filly of Dieppe, had at least fifty men aboard. The 24-year-old Pierre is mentioned on the crew manifest as coming from Chef-Boutonne, capital of the Canton of Deux-Sevres. (1)

Pierre was the son of Mathurin Blais and Francoise Penigaut. Mathurin had a wife previous to Pierre's mother. She was Marie Auchier whom he married on 9 November 1630, at Melleran, which used to be in the Province of Angouleme, but today is found in the Department of Deux-Sevres. In his second marriage on 30 April 1634, Mathurin conquered the heart of Francoise Penigaut. The witnesses to the marriage were Jean Carrier, Denis Richard, Nicolas Blanchard and the "procurer-fiscal" Pierre Alix. Moreover, and this is a rarity, we find the grandfather of Pierre at the ceremony: Jacques, married also to a Penigaud, one Louise, buried at Melleran on 2 December 1629. (2)

Our Ancestor Pierre Blais was raised in the Parish of HANC nearby Melleran, also in Angouleme. The records of this town do not go back beyond 1684, therefore it is not possible to find his baptismal certificate.

In the census of 1667 in New France, Pierre Blais is mentioned for the first time as living on the Ile d'Orleans and having been born about 1640, occupation laborer. Among his bachelor friends living on the Island we might note Jacques Tardif, Martin Poisson and Francois Marceau. (3)

HIS FARM

On 22 June 1667, before the Notary Paul Vachon, Pierre Blais received a concession of land within the limits of the future parish of Saint-Jean. His neighbors were Antoine Poisson and Hyppolyte Thivierge. In 1681 the census taker notes that Pierre owned 4 head of cattle and 15 arpents of cleared land. It was on this farm that he would live for the remainder of his life—33 more years. (4)

HIS FAMILY

Pierre Blais married Anne Perrot on 12 October 1669, at the church of Sainte-Famille on the Island. (5) Anne Perrot, originally from Saint-Sulpice in Paris, was the daughter of Jean and Jeanne Valta. She was a King's Daughter and brought a dowry into the family estimated at 300 livres. From this first union, ten children were born: 8 boys and 2 girls, of whom 4 died at an early age. These four boys founded the family line: Pierre, Antoine, Jacques and Jean. Anne, the mother, died in childbirth on 29 June 1688 and was buried the next day in the cemetery at Saint Jean, at about 45 years of age.

Pierre remained a widower with two young infants: especially poignant was the little Marguerite, born 29 June on her mother's death bed. It was she who would marry Etienne Lamy in 1714. Pierre sought to reorganize his life, so on 18 April 1689 before Notary Paul Vachon, he nominated a guardian for his children, and had an inventory made of his possessions. (6) On the following 5th of June he married Elizabeth Royer at Saint Jean; she was the daughter of Jean and Marie Targer. (7) From this union five children were shown the light of day: a daughter Anne and 4 boys; Francois, Alexis, Louis-Charles and Gabriel. The last one, Gabriel, was born in March 1699 and adopted by Pierre Coquet and his wife Marie Chaperon. Gabriel married at Boucherville on 31 May 1718.

Pierre Blais died suddenly on 16 February 1700 at about 60 years of age. His widow, Elizabeth Royer, married eight months later, it would be the 16th of November, to Robert Pepin at Saint Jean. (8) She followed her husband to Montreal where she lived out the rest of her days. This couple put seven children into the world, then Elizabeth died and was buried on 22 June 1715 at Montreal.

NUMEROUS POSTERITY

Pierre left behind fifteen children, of whom eleven were alive at the time of his death. Alexis, born 8 April 1693, went exploring down the Mississippi; but alas he was killed, along with his companion Laurent Bransard, by the Chicahas and buried on 3 March 1722 at Kaskaskia, where Pere Marquette had founded a mission and where the French built a fort in 1736. (9)

The first descendant of Pierre Blais to enter the clergy was Francois-Xavier-Ludger; born 16 November 1832 at Saint-Pierre de Montmagny, son of Louis Blais, Colonel, and of Marie Genest. After his ordination at Quebec on 10 May 1857, he became Vicar of La Riviere-au-Renard,

Professor at Notre-Dame du Mont-Carmel and Cure at Riviere-du-Loup. It was at Riviere-du-Loup where his dynamism and devotion accomplished important works which still exist. We also take note of Monseigneur Andre-Albert Blais, born at Saint-Vallier on 26 August 1842. He was consecrated a Bishop on 18 May 1890 and directed the Diocese of Rimouski for 28 years. (10)

Michel Blais, grandson of Our Ancestor Pierre, married Francoise Lizotte; as a young man he worked for the Ursuline Nuns of Quebec. In remembrance of those happy days spent in their house as a domestic, they saw fit to give him a gift of "a horse valued at 180 livres for his farm, which was prosperous." (11) . . . It should be remembered that it was not only the fact that Michel raised superb horses but that he had a grateful heart.

Many Canadian descendants of Our Ancestor Pierre Blais, became Blaise, which family had two branches: Des Bergeres de Rigauville and Sansquartier. (12)

With the poet L.J.C. Fiset, we say:
"The centuries have passed, but their noble dust
Will last forever in your grateful hearts!
Only but for them does heaven hear your prayer!
Thus do we celebrate our ancestors!"

BIBLIOGRAPHY

(1) AK   pages 307 - 309
(2) CE   Vol. 53, page 135
(3) CQ   pages 237 - 244 and page 413
(4) CB & DK   22 June 1667
(5) CB & Z   23 September 1669
(6) CB & DK   18 April 1689
(7) CB & AH   1 June 1689
(8) CB & AH   11 November 1700
(9) CX   Vol. I, page 73, Col. b; Vol. V, page 87, Col. a.
(10) DA   page 313
(11) BH   Vol. 2, page 118
(12) CZ   Vol. 7, page 502
      CJ   Vol. VI (1952), page 392

Pierre Blanchet

Chapter 6

Pierre Blanchet

$\mathscr{P}$ierre Blanchet was the ancestor of all the Blanchets in America. He was born at Saint-Omer-de-Rosieres, Diocese of Amiens, in the Province of Picardy. His father's first name was Noel and his mother was Madeleine Valet. Blanchet or Blanquet is the word for the absence of color, namely white.

THE IMMIGRANT

The twenty-five-year-old Pierre was a weaver by trade. He appears for the first time in New France in the census of 1667. He lived as a paid domestic in the home of Simon Lefebre, located on a hillside nearby Notre-Dame-des-Anges, to the east of Quebec. We don't know any details about the term of his indenture, or the reasons that motivated him to come to Quebec about 1665. (1)

AN ADVANTAGEOUS MARRIAGE

Simon Lefebre-Anger had a neighbor thirteen houses down the row, one Guillaume Fournier. Simon introduced his employee Pierre to the Fournier family, who soon came to appreciate his fine qualities. Pierre, in his turn, appreciated their eldest daughter, Marie. To prove the worth of this aspirant for his daughter's hand, Guillaume Fournier entrusted Pierre with the development of a piece of land he owned not far from Charlesbourg. The trial period was successful and the Seigneur of Saint-Joseph gave his fourteen-year-old daughter in marriage. Marie, a flower of the countryside, was, on her mother's (Francoise) side, the great granddaughter of Louis Hebert, the first Canadian settler. (2)

The marriage contract was signed on Sunday 13 October 1669, in the home of the woodworker Jacques de la Roe, in the presence of the Notary Pierre Duquet, as well as the relatives and friends of the Fournier family. Pierre Blanchet did not have any old friends from Picardy with him, but three neighbors and their wives came in from the Riviere-Saint-Charles to be his witnesses. Father Fournier gave his daughter a milk cow and to his newly acquired son-in-law he gave "a house that he owned near Saint Joseph." Pierre for his part took care of his bride's future with the assurance of 400 livres in case of his death and of 200 livres from his estate before any other partition. (3)

The marriage took place in Notre-Dame de Quebec on 17 February 1670, under the supervision of Father Henri de Bernieres. The newlyweds made their first home in the little cabin near Saint Charles which Pierre had furnished while still a bachelor.

THE HAND ON THE PLOW

The land his father-in-law had given him was not very large, but neither did he own any draft animals. After three years of working with axe and mattock, Pierre decided to leave his little home, his shed and his 4 arpents of cleared land. So on 13 October 1671, he went to Quebec and before Notary Romain Becquet he received a concession from Louis Couillard de Lespinay. The description: "26 arpents of fully wooded land, of which 3 arpents front on the Saint Lawrence River to a depth of 40 arpents." This grant was located in the seigneury de la Riviere-du-Sud, up to the Pointe-a-la-Caille, which today is Saint-Thomas de Montmagny. The grant goes on to state that "the charges to the concessionnaire shall consist of 3 silver livres and 3 live capons in rent to the seigneur and one sol in 'cens' for all of the concession." (4)

On 8 October 1671, Pierre gave a three-year lease on his property near Quebec to Etienne Potier. This farmer had to pay him "thirty bushels of good and salable wheat" delivered on the last day in October each year. (5) However, the following autumn Blanchet sold this property to Louis Rouer for the sum of 200 livres, of which 100 was paid in cash. (6)

AN UNWITTING BREECH

On 21 November 1674, Pierre Blanchet guaranteed to underwrite a payment of 21 livres, 7 sols, 6 deniers, owed by his father-in-law to Pierre Normand the toolmaker. In order to avoid seizure of his boat in settlement of the debt, old Fournier agreed to make payments in kind, i.e., four chairs. He defaulted on this too, and on 29 April 1675 the Sovereign Council ordered Pierre to pay the debt plus costs. (7)

Pierre continued to slave away on his farm at Pointe-a-la-Caille, even to expanding his domain by 4 more arpents in frontage. Toward the end of the summer of 1681 the census-taker visited the family, by now consisting of Pierre, his wife and 5 children. Their possessions were recorded as one gun, a half-timbered house, 7 head of cattle and 8 arpents of cultivatable land. His neighbors were Pierre Joncas and Jean Rolandeau (the ancestor of the Laurendeau's). (8) Later on Pierre obtained yet another concession near the river, 5 by 40 arpents, at Saint-Pierre de Montmagny. (9)

But let's take a look at another involuntary breech of the law. To saw a good plank one needs a good log and Pierre was providing Quebec with many good logs. While enjoying the fruit of his silviculture, quite inadvertently one fine day, Pierre wandered onto his neighbor's land and cut some trees. This neighbor was the Seigneur Louis Couillard who lost no time taking Pierre before the Sovereign Council. Pierre pleaded ignorance and stated his willingness to restore that which was not his. The Court ordered him to place in the hands of his accusor "a third of the lumber in question." (10) All this seemed to have been too much for Pierre for the next thing we know he was turned into the Hotel-Dieu, the hospital of Quebec, with a heart attack.

A DECIMATED FAMILY

Today, it is difficult to assess the anguish and suffering brought about by the infant mortality of those times. Pierre and Marie brought 16 children into the world, but only seven survived: Pierre, Pierre-Guillaume, Marie-Madeleine, Jean, Francoise, Simon and Louis. During the one year of 1681, three of the children were taken to the cemetery at Cape Saint Ignace. Then Simon, a sickly unmarried man, disappeared in his thirties. It may be surmised that the Blanchet family did not enjoy good health. It may also be surmised that if our ancestors, like us, dreaded death, they also pinned their hope on life, and with what heroism! (11)

THE HEAVENLY KINGDOM

Old Pierre Blanchet fell gravely ill on 10 April 1709. He sent for the Cure Mesnage, made his confession, received the last Sacraments and told his pastor his last wishes. Pierre, the old churchwarden, gave 6 arpents of land to the parish in order to help pay for the construction of the Church of Saint-Pierre. Then he gave an arpent of river frontage for the priestly instruction of his youngest son, Louis, age 8 years; however, his desires were not fulfilled. (12)

The present Church of Saint-Pierre, built within a few miles of the setting of the first two, is still a magnificent cultural achievement. Canadian historian B. Collins states, "Thanks to its historic value, to the highly classified works of art it holds, it was accepted as a historic monument."

Upon the death of Pierre, the missionary wrote in the

Montmagny parish register, "This 12th day of the month of April in the year 1709 has been buried in the cemetery of the parish Saint Thomas of the Pointe-a-la-Caille by me the undersigned . . . the 'bonhomme' Blanchet, age about 72 years, after having received all the sacraments. A High Mass was sung for him." In the history book of the Blanchet family, they say he was 65 years old. Doubtless he had the appearance of an older man of 72? (13)

The title "bonhomme" must be understood in the full sense of the word. Pierre Blanchet was an honest man, a hard worker who had more heart than learning—he knew not how to write—and a fervent Christian. It is in honor of Pierre Blanchet that the parish was placed under the protection of Saint Peter on 14 June 1713, because Our Ancestor had died at Saint-Pierre de Montmagny. (14)

AN ACCOUNTING

At his death Pierre left no less than 64 arpents of usable land, of which 9 arpents were at Saint-Thomas and 55 at Saint-Pierre. The personal property left by him was valued at 810 livres, 10 sols and 6 deniers. He had 2 big oxen in the stable, one black and the other red; 7 cows; 5 pigs; 4 geese; 7 chickens and a rooster. He had added a room of 40 square feet onto his old half-timbered house at Saint-Thomas, built of the stone of Saint-Pierre. (15) Unfortunately, there was a lien against his estate of 500 livres, owed to Sieur Lotbiniere. This sum was the remainder of a loan Pierre took out on 6 October 1696, in the amount of 1213 livres and 10 sols.

As for his wife Marie Fournier, she put her affairs in order and placed herself under the guardianship of her son Jean. Used up by hard work and the bearing of sixteen children, the lights of her life were extinguished at the age of 60 years. She was buried in January of 1716 at Saint-Pierre. (16)

TO THEIR HONOR

Among the many illustrious descendants of Our Ancestor Blanchet we may take note of two Bishops: Augustin-Magloire (1797 - 1887), first Bishops of Nesqually (Seattle); and Francois-Norbert, first Archbishop of Oregon City (Portland). As a missionary priest to Richiboucton, New Brunswick, Father Francois-Norbert organized a pilgrimage each year to Saint-Anne of the Burnt Church where the Indians and the Acadians met to happily celebrate the Feast Day of Mother Mary. Francois-Xavier Blanchet (1776 - 1830), a physician and a deputy, founded with his friends, the newspaper LE CANADIEN. Jospeh-Goderic Blanchet (1828 - 1890), a physician and politician, was President of the National Assembly. (17)

On 8 December 1973, a third descendant of Our Ancestor was consecrated Bishop of the Cathedral at Gaspe. His Excellency Monseigneur Bertrand Blanchet, born 19 September 1932 at Saint Thomas-de-Montmagny, is the son of Louis and of Alberta Nicole. College Professor, Laureate in Theology and Biology, His Excellency devotes his time and energy now to the service of God and the people of the Gaspe. Thus a new glory to be added to those already in the Blanchet family.

In 1938, the parishoners of Saint Charles Borromeo in Missouri, raised a monument in their cemetery which bore this inscription, "In memory of LOUIS BLANCHET, 'Chasseur,' and Founder of Saint Charles, Missouri, 1769." This Louis-Charles was born on 11 July 1739, from the marriage of Noel Blanchet and Marie-Xainte Fortin, at l'Islet. At the baptism of his first child in 1759, Louis, then 20 years old, had for his first wife, Angelique Lichomchanga, a comely 17-year-old Indian girl. (18)

One branch of the Blanchet family adopted the surname Laforest. No other variant has been recorded. (19)

BIBLIOGRAPHY

(1)	AK	pages 311 - 312
(2)	U	Vol. 2, pages 27 - 31
(3)	CB & Z	13 October 1669
(4)	CB & K	13 October 1671
(5)	CB & CD	8 October 1671
(6)	CB & K	14 November 1672 and 16 July 1690
(7)	BT	Vol. I, page 927
(8)	AY	page 192
(9)	CB & P	21 July 1699 and 1 July 1703
(10)	BT	Vol. II, pages 444 - 446
(11)	BM	Vol. I, page 216
(12)	BF	Vol. 38, pages 735 - 740
(13)	BJ	293 pages, 1946
(14)	BM	Vol. 2, pages 181 - 183
(15)	CB & BL	16 March 1712
(16)	CB & BL	17 & 18 March 1712
(17)	DA	Unknown
(18)	BJ	293 pages, 1946
(19)	CZ	Vol. 7, page 502

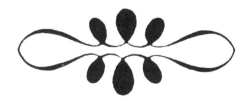

Guillaume Couture

Chapter 7

Guillaume Couture

𝒢uillaume Couture was born in 1617 in the Parish of Saint Godard in Rouen, the capital of Normandy. His late father, also named Guillaume, taught his son to be a carpenter like himself. His mother was Madeleine Mallet and he had a sister Marie. Sometime before 1640 Guillaume left home and hearth and emigrated to Canada. (1)

In 1640 Master Carpenter Couture found his vocation as a "donne," or lay missionary, on the staff of the Jesuit Fathers to the Huron missions in New France. However, in order to assume this status of quasi-priest, he was obliged to renounce his worldly possessions. So while at Quebec on 26 June 1641, before the Notary Martial Piraube, he made an irrevocable gift to his family back in France of "that two-thirds of his father's inheritance left to him, in the parish of Haye Aubray in Normandy." (2)

From this time on, the good Guillaume labored among the Hurons. Father Jogues, on his return to Quebec in 1642 after six years among the Indians, mentioned Couture as one of his traveling companions. (3) We may appreciate some of the difficulties inherent in such traveling when we think of the impenetrable forests, the fragile canoes, the numberless portages, the voracious mosquitoes, not to mention the ever-menacing Iroquois. Up until this time however, Guillaume had not met any Iroquois. Before long his luck would run out.

After 15 days in Quebec, a little band of 40 men went up river to Trois-Rivieres for a few days, outfitting for the return trip to the missions. They set out on the first day of August 1642. After traveling 30 miles, paddling up river against the current, they made camp near Lake Saint-Pierre. The second day out they were attacked by an Iroquois hunting party and straight away the Hurons in the party took off.

"Another Frenchman named Guillaume Couture, seeing the Hurons run away, escaped with them and since he was swift, he was soon beyond capture by the enemy: but remorse seized him for having forsaken his Father (Jogues) and his comrade (Surgeon Rene Goupil, now a canonized Saint). He stopped short, deliberating with himself whether he should go on or go back. He about-faced to return and immediately was confronted by five Iroquois. One of them, a Mohawk Chief, aimed at him with his arquebus. The gun misfired, but the Frenchman in his turn did not miss the Indian—he shot him stone dead on the spot. The other 4 Indians fell on him with the rage of demons. Having stripped him as bare as your hand, they bruised him with heavy blows of their clubs. Then they tore out his fingernails with their teeth—crushing the bleeding ends in order to cause him more pain. Then they pierced one of his hands with a javelin and led him, tied and bound in this sad plight to the place where we were." (4)

The trip into Iroquois territory took 13 days, a true "Way of the Cross." As for himself, Guillaume "suffered almost insupportable torment: hunger, stifling heat, the pain of our wounds, which for not being dressed, became putrid even to breeding worms. Then we encountered a party of 200 Iroquois braves returning from a hunt. They were gleeful on seeing us, they formed two facing lines of 100 on a side, armed themselves with sticks of thorns and made us pass all naked between them down a road of fury and anguish where they let go upon us numerous strong blows." (5)

39

After arriving at their village and being subjected to repeated indignities, "one of these barbarians, having noted that Guillaume Couture, whose hands were torn apart, had not yet lost any of his fingers, seized one of his hands and tried to cut off an index finger with a dull knife, and as he could not succeed therein, he twisted it and in tearing at it, he pulled sinew out of the arm, to the length of a span." (6)

Finally the prisoners were allowed to live and their tortures stopped because the Mohawks believed that they could be useful in trade for making peace. Father Jogues and Rene Goupil were kept in a small distant camp but the Indians sent Guillaume to a larger village. Here this courageous young man was adopted by an old squaw who had lost her brave in battle. Thus he was protected and treated as a member of the tribe. One can sum up this period of disruption in the life of Guillaume Couture thusly: "Vigorous, active, indefatigable, able to stand the worst misery, yet always content, habituated in all the arts dear to the savages, excellent shot, swift runner, capable of traveling the woods or paddling a canoe, this Norman, intrepid as are all Normans, was not slow to emulate the spirit of his new companions. He conformed to their ways, learned their language so much and so well that they ended up by admitting him into the councils of the nation. While his friends deplored their lot, Couture was enthroned in dignity in the midst of the Indian Sachems." (7)

In the spring of 1645, after three years of captivity, Couture saw the arrival of an Indian who had been captured but sent back by the French Governor de Montmagny. This Iroquois brought a message that Ononthio was desirous of negotiating a peace. Two Mohawk delegates were sent back with Guillaume Couture to Trois-Rivieres to parlay. As for his homecoming, "As soon as he was recognized everyone threw their arms around him, looking on him as a man resurrected from the dead . . . ." (8)

Guillaume, now a free man, returned with the emissaries in order to make a peace treaty acceptable to the Mohawk tribe. Returning in the spring of 1646 he was celebrated everywhere as the artisan of peace. However, he would not be content until he had revisited the Huron missions and so he went back to them with Father Pijart.

Evidently the good Guillaume had learned the Indian dialects during his trips and his captivity. He was a precise interpreter, a faithful companion to the missionaries, and a powerful ambassador of the young colony accredited to the American Indians. In 1646, the Jesuit Father Buteux put on a festival in honor of Couture at Trois-Rivieres, and gave him the Indian name of Achirra, to their great delight. (9)

The government of that time was forever calling on the services of Couture: in 1657, in 1661, in 1663 and in 1666 they sent him to Albany, New Netherlands. In 1665 Guillaume accompanied Father Henri Nouvel to the territory of the Papinachois, along the north coast. Then on another expedition with some missionaries he was shipwrecked not far from a point of land nearby Rimouski, called the Pointe-au-Pere. (10)

FATHER OF A PEOPLE

Guillaume Couture asked to be relieved of his vows as a lay missionary and subsequently, on 26 April 1646, the Journal of the Jesuits mentioned that the Council of the Order announced that it had unanimously approved of Guillaume's marriage. It was on 18 November 1649 that he married Anne Esmard. (11) She was baptized on 22 October 1627, in Saint Andre de Niort, Poitou. She was the daughter of the late Jean and Marie Bineau. Anne had two sisters in Canada: Barbe, wife of Gilles Michel dit Taillon, and after him, of Olivier Letardif; and Madeleine, wife of Zacharie Cloutier. The wedding of Guillaume and Anne took place in the house of Couture, at Pointe Levy, in the presence of Father Jean LeSeur, Chaplain of the Hospital-

41

liers of Quebec. The couple engendered ten children: 6 boys and 4 girls.

Today their offspring are very numerous. However, many have forgotten their heritage because the name Couture has been lost among them. Thus, the descendants of Jean Baptiste are called Lamonde and those of Eustache are known as Bellerive. Son Louis, baptized in 1654, would go down the Mississippi and all trace of him would be lost. The daughters married into the grand families of Cote, Marsolet, Couillard, Vezier and Bourget. Three of the boys joined in marriage in one Huard family.

THE RESPECTED CITIZEN

On 15 May 1647, Guillaume Couture was granted a concesson, 5 arpents of river frontage by 40 arpents deep. He cleared and settled this land at Pointe Levy and it became the ancestral home. (12) His first neighbor was Francois Bissot; their property was separated by a brook. The Jesuits had some land nearby to the east on which was built a modest shelter called the "Cabin of the Fathers." The first Mass was probably celebrated there on 12 April 1648 by Father Pierre Bailloquet. Then in 1667, they built a beautiful church on the land of Bissot, where the first priest in residence was the Abbot Philippe Boucher. It was known as Saint Joseph up until 1690. The second neighbor of Guillaume, about 1651, was Charles Cadieu dit Courville, the fellow who operated an eel fishery. (13)

Guilluame also had a lot on which he built a house of 24 feet frontage by 40 feet deep, in the Rue Sous-le-Fort in the lower town of Quebec City, on the Place Royale. (14)

The census of 1667 tells us that he had 20 arpents under cultivation and 6 animals. During his long absences his tenant farmer Guillaume Durand looked after things for him.

As it was necessary to rally to the defense of the colony when called upon to do so, about 1666 our Guillaume was named a Captain of Militia on the Lauzon coast, a very important responsibility at that time. In 1681 he had four field cannon in his force and it was reported that in 1690, at the age of 73, the Captain and his men opposed the advance of Phipps and his troops along the Lauzon coast. This Captain of Militia, because he could also read and write, was required to carry out the orders and proclamations of the Governor, command the troops, preside over census enumerations and convene citizen assemblies.

Moreover Guillaume was Chief Magistrate of the same territory up until his death. We know that Our Ancestors were quite capable of committing misdemeanors and it was the duty of the Magistrate to reconcile problems and differences before they went up to the Sovereign Council. The Magistrate became, in most of the litigations, judge, prosecutor, jury and arbiter. He even performed the duty of what today would be called the coroner. (15)

TO THEIR GLORY

It was the mother who was the first to go. Anne Esmard was buried at Levis on 18 November 1700. Then the patriarch Couture entered the hospital of Quebec on 31 March 1701, where he died the following 4th of April. The Notary Lepailleur took an inventory of his belongings on 14 November that same year. (16)

Let us not forget that Guillaume Couture, in spite of all the service he rendered to the colony of New France, did not ask for nor did he receive any title of nobility or special privilege. He had only that given by the King of France to all those who had 10 or more children—a family allowance of 300 livres annually, and even that ended in 1681. During his lifetime Guillaume thought only of others; the indigenous, the French, his children. He had but one goal: Peace and Charity.

In 1947 a great celebration marked the 300th anniversary of Guillaume Couture at Pointe Levy. On this occasion the *Biography of Heroes,* by Joseph-Edmond Roy was republished. (7)

In addition to the surnames of Bellerive and Lamond, the family names of Crevier, De la Cressonniere and Lafresnaie were adopted by some descendants of Our Ancestor. (17)

BIBLIOGRAPHY

(1)	V	Vol. II, pages 163 - 166
(2)	CO	160 pages 1884
(3)	AV	1647
(4)	DB	1647, page 21 - 29
(5)	CM	Guillaume Couture, pages 115 - 151
(6)	DB	1647, page 47
(7)	CO	160 pages 1884
(8)	DB	1645, page 23
(9)	CM	Guillaume Couture, page 130
(10)	BM	Vol. I, pages 197 - 200
(11)	CB & H	18 November 1649 and 20 August 1641, 16 September 1653, 7 September 1658, 26 August 1659
(12)	CB & BB	4 November 1647
(13)	BC	Vol. I, pages 445 - 447
(14)	CB & Z	28 May 1665 and 22 April 1668, 5 July 1682
(15)	BT	Vol. I, pages 417, 438, 624 - 625, 656 - 658, 924, 926, 943 - 944, 957 - 958 and 969 Vols. II, III & V, many references.
(16)		Langlois, Michel. Deces inscrits au Registre des Malades de L'Hotel-Dieu de Quebec (1689 - 1722).
(17)	CZ	Volume 7, page 513

Grégoire Deblois

Chapter 8

Gregoire Deblois

$\mathcal{T}$he name Deblois harks back to the time of a celebrated town in France—Blois, the glorious gateway to the chateaus of the Loire, and of a saintly man, Charles de Blois, Duke of Brittany, writer and soldier, who died on the field of honor, nearby Sainte-Anne-d'Aurey, on the 29th of September, 1364.

Today we direct our attention to the ancestor, Gregoire Deblois, father of so many dignified descendants who bear either of his names, GREGOIRE as well as DEBLOIS.

A DIFFICULT CROSSING

It was on 3 March 1657, at La Rochelle, that Gregoire Deblois indentured himself in order to get to Canada. Notary Pierre Moreau signed him into the service of the merchants Grignon, Gaigneux and Masse, for three years' work as a prison guard in Quebec. In return, he was to get free passage and the assurance of a salary of 70 livres for each of these years.

A ship named LES ARMES d'AMSTERDAM appeared in the harbor of La Rochelle one fine day in mid-April. This 250-ton Dutchman, armed with 10 cannon and 6 blunderbusses, was chartered by her owner, Jacob Gillensen, to the three merchants named above, who then signed on a French crew for the passage.

Captain Jean Guyonneau, underway about the 10th of April, set his sails for New France. Bad weather took charge; he lost his rudder and almost lost his ship as well. Steering by sail, stricken and belabored, he barely made port at Limerick, Ireland. After a month of refitting, the ship put to sea again, but hardly 24 hours later her seams opened. With the hull filling fast, an anchorage was made off a lee shore at Quilmar. By June 28th, repairs were once more completed; so for a third time these men set out to brave the North Atlantic. After seven storm-tossed weeks, on August 20th, the unlucky Dutch caravelle finally put into Quebec. For Gregoire Deblois, this year of 1657 would be the start of a new life. (1)

ESTABLISHMENT

It is possible that Ancestor Deblois was a prison guard at Quebec but there is no proof of it. The next news we have of him comes on 2 February 1660, at Chateau Richer, when his name appears on the list of those confirmed by Mgr de Laval. It was on the feast day of the Purification of Mary that 173 people received the Sacrament: Gregoire was 17th in line; Louis Joliet, the future discoverer of the Mississippi, is mentioned as the 132nd. (2)

On 10 January 1661, Gregoire Deblois received a land grant from Seigneur Lauzon-Charnay, consisting of three arpents of river frontage in the Parish of Sainte-Famille, Ile d'Orleans. His neighbors were Jean Lehoux and Elie-Joseph Gaultier. He planted his first crop that spring but, on 25 July, he sold his land to Nicolas Gendron for 80 livres. (3) Then in June of the next year, 1662, Gregoire obtained a concession of 3 arpents of river frontage from the widow d'Aillebout, who mistakenly believed that she was giving him a piece of land in Argentenay, Ile d'Orleans. On 23 June 1664, she was supposed to have cleared this title before a notary. (4) Here Gregoire built himself a cabin by the river shore and the census of 1667 tells us that he had 8 arpents of cleared land.

On 8 March 1668, before Notary Paul Vachon at Quebec, Mgr de Laval conceded 3 arpents of river frontage to each of three men: Francois Rousseau, Francois Dupont and Gregoire Deblois. This was choice property, on the north coast of the Ile d'Orleans facing the Church of Sainte-

Anne-de-Beaupre across the river. In the case of Deblois, it was the same land he was already farming; the grant merely confirmed his presence and finally gave him a clear and unencumbered title. (5) We know that by 1681 he had 6 head of cattle and 18 arpents of land. According to the Villenueve map of 1689, his neighbors were Francois Dupont and Robert Coutard; Gregoire had built a house and two barns on his property.

After having spent five years getting the lay of the land, i.e. its climate, its forests, its great river full of fish, and experiencing the exigencies of farming, Gregoire thought it was high time he settle down to a solid and steady way of life. He courted Francoise, newly arrived in the country, the daughter of Robert Viger and Perrine Remillard. The Viger family was from the Parish of Doue-la-Fontaine in Anjou. The pair soon decided to get married, but first the contract! So, Gregoire Deblois, son of Francois and Marguerite Papelone, of the town Champagne-Mouton, in Poitou, took himself and his future companion to the house of the Notary Audouart, where a contract was signed on 3 August 1662. (6) Thus did the Poitevan and Angevin, on 11 September 1662, in the Parish of Chateau Richer, unite their future days. Their own Parish of Sainte-Famille, although founded in 1661, had no church until 1669; then it was built under the direction of Father Dufrost de la Jemmerais. It was at Sainte-Famille that eight children were born and would grow up: of these eight, Joseph, Jean, Germain, Jean-Baptiste and Marie were married in the home parish; as for Reine, the wife of Xiste Lereau (L'Heureau), her marriage took place at Saint-Francois on the Ile d'Orleans. (7)

The family suffered two bereavements: son Guillaume, baptized on 21 March 1668, was buried in April 1681, at 13 years of age; son Charles Francois, born 22 October 1670 and died on 30 November 1689, at 19 years of age. His remains were taken overland, the river being not yet frozen, to the cemetery at the Hotel-Dieu, in Quebec. But there were so many family joys to erase these troubles; the marriage of the six children united Gregoire and Francoise to the families Rosseau, Dupont, L'Heureau and Pelletier as well as enlarging the circle of their friends. (8)

DEPARTING CHRISTIAN SOULS

Work became more and more arduous for Gregoire. He was about 73 years old and his hair white with age. Around him he could count 13 lively grandchildren, each a blessing to him. However, in the fall of 1705, the bells tolled the hour of his departure and Our Ancestor left his adopted land for the eternity of Heaven. After a religious ceremony at the Church of Sainte-Famille, he was buried the 24th of November on the Ile d'Orleans.

On 23 February 1706, in the home of son-in-law Xiste Lereau, Notary Etienne Jacob recorded the donation of Francoise Viger, the widow Deblois. Each child was to receive an equal share of her land, but which heir received which share was decided by lottery. "Five tickets of equal size . . . the said tickets containing the name of each of the inheritors, all put in a hat, and after each drawing again shaken up." Later on that day, contracts of sale recorded by the same notary showed that the patrimony would remain with the brothers Germain and Jean and finally it would be Jean owning all of the family land. More than ten generations of his successors have lived on this farm, each adding to its history, improving the site and maintaining the fertility of the land. (9)

As for Francoise Viger, "mater familias," she continued to live among her children at Saint-Francois on the Ile d'Orleans until—seven years after her husband's death—she too died and was buried beside him on 23 March 1712.

AN IMPRESSIVE HARVEST

Let us gather a few particulars about this impressive harvest of remarkable children.

Pierre Antoine Deblois, born in 1815, was a senator and, as a former mayor, left his name on a street in Beauport. His sister, Josephine, married The Honorable Rene Edouard Caron, Lieutenant Governor of the Province of Quebec.

Joseph Gregoire, born at Saint Valentin on 5 August 1833, from the marriage of Joseph and Anastasie Remillard, is known as the Father of the Canadians of Lake Superior. He was a miner at Norwick, Michigan; also a builder of a quay at Superior City and a lumberjack, joiner and carpenter as well. In 1856, Joseph constructed the first pier in the old port of Duluth; in 1859 he became a businessman at Houghton, Michigan; in 1865, the owner of a shipyard on Portage Lake in Houghton County and 7 years later he owned a sawmill at nearby Lake Linden where he built a factory for making wood doors and frames. For a time, Lake Linden was called Gregoireville and even had a French school. (10)

Charles N. Deblois obtained a Doctorate in Medicine at Laval University in 1892. He founded the Sanitorium Deblois at Trois-Rivieres and published many medical papers, openly respected in the United States and Europe. Doctor Deblois even dabbled in antiquaries: in 1889, he built the Chateau Deblois at Trois-Rivieres on the model of the great chateaus of France. (11)

Mother Leoni, Foundress of the Little Sisters of the Holy Family, was the daughter of Emilie Gregoire (Deblois) and of Jospeh Paradis. (12)

His Excellency, Monseigneur Paul Gregoire, Archbishop of Montreal is equally a direct descendant of the humble ancestor Gregoire Deblois.

> "Long ago did France, upon our shores
>   Cast her immortal seed;
> And we in our turn to try,
>   Have built New France, indeed."
>
> (Louis Frechette)

BIBLIOGRAPHY

(1)	AN	1962, 90 pages
(2)	BF	Vol. 47, pages 139 - 146
(3)	CB & H	25 July 1661
(4)	DG	pages 59, 64, 540
(5)	CB & DK	10 March 1668
(6)	CB & H	3 August 1662
(7)	CQ	pages 74 - 76
(8)	AN	1962, 90 pages
(9)	CB & AS	23, February 1706
(10)	BF	Vol. 47, pages 316 - 317
(11)	CJ	Vol. 52, page 383
(12)	X	Vol. III, pages 1516 - 1517
(12)	BS	pages 22 - 29
	CB & F	8 July 1663 and 3 August 1670

Vue de Québec – 1759

Antoine Dionne

Chapter 9

Antoine Dionne

That autumn a boat crossed the river carrying a small body. After the Ceremony of the Angels, Father Thomas Morel wrote in his register:

"The 28th November 1664 Andre Dionne son of Antoine Ivory his father and mother inhabitants of the island age of three years has been buried in the cemetery of Chateau Richer by me Morel priest of Seminary of Quebec while carrying out my religious duties." (1)

This child was not born in Canada. If Father Morel had written the date of birth of Andre and his parish in the record, what a service he would have rendered to the researchers of today! Antoine Dionne and Catherine Ivory arrived in Canada about 1661.

TWO DIONNE BROTHERS

The Dionne brothers, Jean and Antoine, came to New France together. They bore the family name Guyonne and the surname Sansoucy. By what promise or contract did they cross the Atlantic? It is impossible to say. We are even ignorant as to the names of their parents and that of the French province of origin. As for their name, Guyonne may be changed very quickly to Dionne.

Sometime before 14 July 1662 Jean obtained a concession in the "second rang" in the fief of Charney-Lirec on the Ile d'Orleans. This land grant was 2 arpents in frontage by 63 in depth; his neighbors were Pierre Chalut and Maurice

Crepeau.

At Beauport on the 5th of June 1663 Jean agreed to be godfather to Anne Chalut, daughter of Pierre and of Marie Bonin. At the same time, Anne Fosse, wife of Francois La Raue, acted as godmother. Again on 3 August 1665 at Quebec, Jean signed as godfather to his niece Anne Dionne.

Jean Dionne dit Sansoucy, resident of Beauport, must have become fed up with life on the farm because on 7 November 1674 Romain Becquet notarized a sale to Jean LeSueur of the land acquired in 1662. From that time on, we lose all trace of him.

A RESTLESS ANCESTOR

Brother Antoine Dionne was not the type of stubborn worker who sticks to one plot of land without ever looking elsewhere. In fact, his whole life seemed to have been spent in buying, selling and exchanging property, while moving his family around. (2)

For several years he lived on his brother's farm in Saint Pierre Parish, Ile d'Orleans. Nevertheless, Antoine did have his own place: On 2 March 1665 he bought a tiny farm, 2 arpents in frontage, from Jean Mourier. It was bordered by the farms of Rene Cosset and Laurent Benoist. (3)

The record shows that in 1666 he was living between neighbors Michel Chartier the netmaker and Rene Valet. The following year we are told that the 26-year-old Antoine Guyonne and Catherine Ivory, age 22 years, owned 8 arpents of cleared land and one head of cattle: their neighbors were Thomas LeSeuer and Pierre Chalut. For awhile he cultivated the farm of his brother Jean; then he exchanged his own land that he had bought in 1665 with Jean Vallee, for another piece three arpents wide, bordered by Jean Guy and Joachim Martin. On this site he had 6 arpents of cleared land and here he brought his family and possessions to live for at least six years. (4)

This farm, in the future Parish of Saint-Pierre, situated at Longue-Pointe, had a house, barn and stable, but nevertheless he sold it to Jean Leclerc dit le Bouteleau on 10 October 1675. (5) One fine day, Jean up and left in order to go to the Parish of Saint-Francois, remitting the land back to Dionne. On 3 November 1679, Antoine sold it again, this time to Jean Guy, his neighbor. (6)

It was on 18 October 1675 that Antoine bought a 3-arpent-wide strip of land from Joseph-Ozanni Nadeau dit Lavigne at Sainte-Famille; the neighbors were Jean Moreau and Philippe Paquet. (7)

According to the census of 1681 the Dionne family was fairly well off, having 25 arpents of usable land, 3 head of cattle and a musket. His son-in-law Bertrand Laisne, husband of daughter Anne, lived under the same roof: even more entangling was the fact that he had mortgaged the farm to the said Laisne. (8) By now Antoine was 45 years old and finally he stayed put. In 1689 the engineer Villeneuve made a map of the area and it shows this land of Dionne, located between that of Nicholas Paquin and of Michel Montambault dit Leveille. Here one finds the cradle of the Dionne family of America. (9)

In 1702 Antoine had a stone house 30 feet wide with a chimney, a shed, a stable and 30 arpents of land under cultivation. In 1709 the cartographer Gedeon Catalogne mentions Dionne as the proprietor of this land.

FROM QUEBEC TO LAUZON

Even though Antoine remained in possession of the family hearth, it is not to say that he always stayed there. He bought a lot, 20 feet in frontage, on the river in the lower town of Quebec; here he would build a house in 1679. (10)

Henri Brau, resident of the coast of Lauzon, made a deal

with Antoine Dionne: Brau would cede a piece of land 4 arpents by 40, with fishing rights, in exchange for the place that Antoine had in Quebec. (11) Antoine made use of his fishing rights; he marketed eels to Lucien Boutteville, a merchant of Quebec, from whom Antoine had borrowed money. (12) Antoine had many talents: farming, trading, carpentry and even eel fishing.

SIX OUT OF TWELVE

The Dionne couple had twelve children. These six died young: Antoine, Marie-Anne, Marguerite, two named Catherine and one unnamed. Five girls married into the families of Laisne dit Laliberte, Lenormand, Benoit, Gobeil and Michaud. A single son, Jean, kept the Dionne name alive. On the 2nd of August 1694, when 24 years old, Jean married Marie-Charlotte Mignot dit Chatillon at Chateau Richer. She was the daughter of Jean and of Louise Cloutier and the sister of Therese Mignot, the wife of my ancestor Nicholas Lebel. (13)

Like father like son. Jean took after his father early in life; while still a minor of 15. Before 1685, he obtained a concession in the parish of Saint-Jean, Ile d'Orleans. Five years later he sold it to Vincent Chretien, Jr. (14) At 18, Jean bought the farm of Pierre Boucher of Saint Famille. (15) Then Notary Etienne Jacob tells us that on 26 March 1701 he turned the same piece over to Nicolas Asselin. From 1700 on, he lived on the east coast in Riviere Ouelle, today's Kamouraska. (16)

GIVEN A LONG LIFE

I shall pass over without comment the complicated disputes which took place between the Dionne children on the subject of supporting their old parents. In those days everyone was poor; old age pensions and the beneficence of today had not yet been invented. It appears that, instead of staying in the family, the Dionne couple made their donation to Barthelemy Gobiel. (17) Catherine Ivory died sometime after 1709 and then Antoine ended his days in the home of his son-in-law Gobiel. He was buried on Christmas Day 1721, over 80 years old.

In the register of receipts and expenditures of the parish of Sainte Anne-de-Beaupre in 1664, we find an enigmatic entry: "in the name of San Soucy one minot of wheat." Might it have referred to the ancestor Dionne dit San Soucy? He could have made a gift to the Church of Sainte Anne-de-Beaupre at this time, however this surname was also used by his brother Jean and by Gabriel Rouleau. (18)

LIKE THE STARS IN HEAVEN

The descendants of Antoine Dionne have furnished some brilliant men in nearly every sphere of society: big businessmen, deputies, professionals, etc. The first notary of Sainte Anne-de-Pocatiere was Joseph. He received his Commission on 20 February 1743. Narcisse E. Dionne (1848 - 1917), doctor and advertising executive, left his name for posterity as biographer and librarian to the Legislative Assembly. Many priests, numerous religious brothers and sisters also carried this name with pride; for example, Monseigneur Gerard Dionne, after 4 February 1975, Auxiliary Bishop of Sault-Saint-Marie.

Forty-five years have passed since an extraordinary event filled the pages of the newspapers, not only of Canada, but of the entire world. On 28 May 1934, the Dionne quintuplets were born at Callander, Ontario; the daughters of Oliva and of Elzire Legros. In the memory of man, it was the first time that quintuple identical twins, like five new stars, had survived; thanks to modern science and the help of Doctor A.R. Defoe. Six days after their premature birth the babies weighed only 11.5 pounds total. (19) Emilie and Marie are now dead. We can render homage here to their parents who did everything to educate them in the mother tongue according to the principles of our Holy Mother Church. The father of the quints died at the hospital in North Bay on 15 November 1979 at the age of 76.

In addition to the original name of Guyonne, from which Dionne evolved, later generations adopted the name Dianne as well. (20)

BIBLIOGRAPHY

(1) CF   1661 - 1690
(2) BF   Vol. 55, pages 53 - 60
(3) CB & DK   2 March 1665
(4) CB & F   20 September 1669
(5) CB & CD   19 October 1675
(6) CB & DK   3 November 1679
(7) CB & Z   18 October 1675 and 14 August 1681
(8) CB & CD   1 February 1680
(9) CQ   pages 10, 11, 13, 25, 64, 150, 152, 358, 366, 382, etc.
(10) CB & CD   11 February 1678
(11) CB & CD   2 September 1679
(12) CB & CD   15 April 1680
(13) CZ   Vol. I, page 196; Vol. III, pages 419 - 420
(14) CB & DK   22 March 1689
(15) CB & DK   10 March 1687
(16) BF   Vol. 54, page 78
(17) CB & AH   15 March 1709 and
     AS   26 March 1709
(18) D   Manuscript Records
(19) CW   pages 37 - 48
(20) CZ   page 524
     CB & P   5 April 1702, 28 October 1702
     CX   Vol. IV, page 57, col. c; page 72, col. a; Vol. V, page 85, col. b.
     BM   Vol. 26, pages 177 - 178

Vue de Québec – 1832

Julien Fortin

Chapter 10

Julien Fortin
dit
Bellefontaine

*I*t was at Saint Cosme-de-Vair on 9 February 1621, on the border of the old Province of Perche in France, where Our Ancestor Julien Fortin was baptized. He had a sister, Helene, and three brothers; he was the half brother of eight other children by Julienne Guillemin. His father, also a Julien and the son of Simon, was a butcher by trade. Young Julien lost his mother on 24 November 1628, when he was but seven years old. She was the daughter of Gervais Lavye and had married Julien senior on 26 November 1618 in the Parish of Notre Dame.

ARRIVAL IN CANADA

Doctor Robert Giffard, proprietor of the Seigneury of Beauport in New France, returned to France for a visit in 1634 and stayed at the celebrated Inn of the Cheval Blanc. It so happened that this hostelry was owned by Gervais Lavye, the maternal grandfather of Julien. Our future colonist was about 13 years old and fascinated with the stories told by Seigneur Giffard about life in Canada. Robert went back to Canada, but returned to France in 1650 on a recruiting mission. As a result, many of the local citizens of Perche decided to emigrate in company with Giffard, Julien included.

The 29-year-old Julien took himself to the port of Dieppe in Normandy, embarked for New France and spent three long months at sea because of head winds. The ship finally arrived at Quebec by the end of the summer of 1650. Disembarking with Julien Fortin were passengers Simon Rocheron and his sister Marie, a carpenter named Rouillard, the tailor Claude Bouchard, Simon Lereau, the ancestor of all the L'Hereux, and many other emigrants. (1)

AN ACTIVE AND PROSPEROUS COLONIST

Arriving in the country after two months of suffering at sea, Julien Fortin dit Bellefontaine, lost no time getting started. Perhaps he had some money set aside, or some economic resources on which he could draw, because he bought a prime piece of waterfront property just in front of Sainte Anne-de-Beaupre on 26 December 1650; a fortuitous Christmas present to himself. He sold it to Robert Caron on 27 March 1654 for the sum of 500 livres.

On 23 August 1657 Julien became part owner of both the Seigneury of Beaupre and of the Ile d'Orleans. The seller was Sieur Charles de Lauzon-Charny, Commandant-General of New France, the son of Jean and Louise Giffard. Our ancestor was obviously well connected. Julien paid 700 livres in beaver pelts for this fiefdom. On 11 February 1662, he sold it all to Mgr de Laval for 750 livres, but not without reward. (2)

On 4 June 1659 our prosperous Julien was given a concession at Cape Tourmente of 6 arpents of river frontage by a league and a half in depth. (3) Today this territory goes by the name of "The Fortin Coast". The census of 1666, 1667 and 1681 tell us that he lived there. In 1667 he had two domestics in his employ, Leonard and Francois Jarivet; he had 8 arpents of cleared land and 7 beasts in the stable and he would live in Saint Joachim until his death.

Julien also owned lot number 149, 12 arpents on the Saint Lawrence River by 42 arpents in depth. He purchased this land, located in the territory known as LaPetite Riviere de Saint Francois in Charlevoix county, for the sum of 280 livres from Pierre Laforest dit Labranche and his wife Charlotte Anne Godin, daughter of Elie and of Esther Ramage. (4)

AN INVOLVED CITIZEN

On 2 February 1660, the Feastday of the Purification of Mary, Julien was confirmed at Chateau-Richer by Mgr Francois de Laval, Bishop of Quebec.

On 6 October of the same year, before Father Francois Le Mercier and Churchwarden Joseph Mace-Gravel, Julien made a gift to the Church of Notre-Dame de la Visitation at Chateau Richer, of 50 livres and a little wooden house.

The following year, 6 October 1661, he testified by deposition before the court on the subject of the Iroquois ravages: the sacking of the farms of Jean Picard, the widow Caron and Claude Bouchard, as well as the massacre of six people, among whom was Louis Guimond. (5)

Two gifts were recorded in the register of receipts and expenditures of the church of Saint Anne: 27 January 1665 "given by bellefontaine 20 S," that is to say one livre; and "received from bellefontaine two minots of wheat," early in 1676. (6)

As recorded by Notary Romain Becquet on 18 August 1680, Julien "gave to Pierre Voyer, Guillaume Boucher and Felix Auber, Wardens of Chateau-Richer, for the Churches of Chateau-Richer and Sainte-Anne, a house situated at Chateau-Richer nearby the church, with a bakehouse at one end, bordered on one side by Thomas (name illegible), for the use of the two churches equally . . . the said donation made to the said churches because of the great devotion that he has for them." (7)

Thus we see Our Ancestor Fortin as a man of generous faith and also of sincere attachment to Mary and Sainte Anne.

THE FATHER OF A LARGE FAMILY

On 11 November 1652 Julien married the 17 year old Genevieve Gamache, daughter of Nicholas Gamache dit Lamarre and of Jacqueline Cadot. They were from Sainte-Illiers, Diocese of Chatres in the Beauce region of France. Present at the ceremony were the father of Genevieve, Nicholas Gamache, the Sieur Le Tardif, Louis Gagne and Claude Auber. Father Ragueneau, SJ, blessed the marriage, which took place in the home of Louis Gagne, at Cape Tourmente, which was at that time within the limits of Sainte Anne parish. The contract of marriage had been made previously at the house of Toussaint on the Cape, on 22 August 1652, by Notary Claude Auber. (8)

On 21 October 1654 there was great joy around the Fortin hearth for a daughter, Barbe, was born. On the 10th of the following month Father Paul Ragueneau went to the home of the said Bellefontaine on the Beaupre coast, to carry out the baptismal ceremony. The Grand Senechal of the country, Jean de Lauzon, acted as godfather. Barbe Aymont, wife of Sieur Le Tardif, as godmother, gave the gift of her first name to the baby. Then, another baby came along just about every 23 months, until 15 June 1677, when the last was born. They were Charles, Eustache (later to be a major of militia at Cape Saint Ignace), Jacques, Genevieve, Joseph, Marie-Ann, Julien, Pierre, Louis, Jean and Marguerite the youngest. A total of 8 boys and 4 girls, all baptized at Sainte Anne-de-Beaupre.

If great joy accompanies a large family so must there be a few crosses to bear. In 1687 Julien and Louise, ages 20 and 16 respectively, died in the flower of their youth. Some months later, on 10 August the same year, Pierre Gagnon, the husband of Barbe the eldest, was buried at Sainte Anne. All three were victims of epidemics of scarlet fever and the measles, which swept the region that year; then the small pox epidemic of 1702-03 took Marie-Anne, Genevieve and Joseph. (9)

A MIRACLE OF SAINTE ANNE

In the year 1667, Father Thomas Morel set himself to the task of recording the miracles accomplished through the intercession of Sainte Anne of the Little Cape. The following paragraph tells of a prodigious event that happened to the Fortin family in 1666.

"Barbe fortin, daughter of Julien fortin belle fontaine habitant of Beaupre age of twelve years or about attack by a pleurisy and in danger of death, having been recommended to Sainte Anne by her father and mother who made a vow and novena to her straight away received a perfect cure at the end of the novena." (10)

FAREWELL CHRISTIAN FRIENDS

We do not know the exact date of death of Our Ancestor Fortin. We do know that on 18 June 1689, Julien was godfather to his granddaughter Marie, the daughter of Genvieve and of Noel Gagnon. Then nothing more! At the second marriage of Barbe to Pierre Lessard on 16 April 1690, Julien did not sign as a witness, so it is reasonable to assume that he died between those two dates, some say in September 1687. The colony had lost a great man. (11)

Genevieve Gamache continued to live from the inheritance of her late husband, but she would end her days in the home of her son Charles at l'Islet, not far from the fief of her brother Nicholas Gamache dit Lamarre. She was buried at Notre Dame de BonSecours, at l'Islet, 5 Nobember 1709. (12)

On 17 August 1777, a third generation Fortin was ordained a priest. Jean-Marie was the Cure of Sault-au-Ricollet, of Lotbiniere, of Sainte Foy and of Saint Jean, Ile d'Orleans. He died at the Hospital General of Quebec on 9 December 1829 and was buried at Saint Jean. (13)

In addition to the surname Bellefontaine, some descendants of Julien Fortin also took the names of Hermel and Paris. (14)

BIBLIOGRAPHY

(1)	AE	Cahier Special F, 82 pages
(2)	I	pages 195, 199, 206, 207
(3)	I	Saint Joachim, page 92
(4)	CB & AS	12 March 1685
(5)	BM	Vol. 25, pages 38 - 40
(6)	D	Archival manuscript
(7)	E	Tablette 19, 9, No. 390
(8)	CB & F	22 August 1652 and 23 October 1652. Additionally, 6 October 1660, 31 October 1661, 13 November 1662, 25 June 1663, 2 June 1664, 6 July, 1664, 10 February 1666, 13 January 1670, 3 August 1670, 13 January 1667 and 18 August 1680.
(9)	AF	Manuscript 1973, 89 pages
(10)	D	P-14, b1, doc 410, XVIII
(11)	AE	Cahier Special F, 82 pages
(12)	BN	MON CLOCHER, 1964, pages 38 - 40
(13)	DA	1893
(14)	CZ	Volume 7, page 530
	CB & H	30 September 1659 and 6 October 1661
	CB & BW	24 February 1658, 15 October 1658 and 10 October 1659
	CB & CD	2 February 1667 and 18 March 1667
	CB & DK	16 January 1674, 7 January 1676 and 27 January 1676
	X	Vol. III, pages 1564 - 1565
	AG	pages 25, 32, 51, 53, 60, 62, 81, 82, 133, 144, 148, 159, 160, 164
	AX	pages 28, 109, 286
	CE	Volume 16 (1935 - 36) page 6
		Barbe Fortin as a pensionnaire at the Ursuline home in Quebec.

Vue de Québec - 1840

Jean Gagnon

Chapter 11

The Gagnon Ancestors
by Gabriel U. Gagnon

The Gagnons of Canada have four ancestors who came from France. More precisely, they came from the towns of Tourouvre and Ventrouze in the tiny Province of Perche, just south of Normandy. Initially, the brothers Mathurin, Jean and Pierre lived on a farm, in a little village called La Gagnonniere in the forest of Perche, between Tourouvre and Ventrouze. Their parents, Pierre Gagnon and Renee Roger, were tenants of his father and mother Barnabe and Francoise Crest, who had bought the farm from Gervais Roger and Marion Aubert on 28 December 1565. One should also note that they owned an inn on the same spot. Robert, son of Jean Gagnon and of Marie Geffroy, came from Ventrouze. (1)

ESTABLISHING THEMSELVES IN CANADA

In 1635, one finds the three brothers, Mathurin, Jean and Pierre at Quebec where they opened a shop, 60 by 24 feet, on the Rue Saint-Pierre in the lower town. Their business partner was Mace Gravel who married Marguerite, daughter of the sister of these three first ancestors, on the 1st of May 1644 at Quebec. Later they sold this business to Pierre Pellerin on 9 October 1668.

Afterwards they went to Chateau-Richer to settle down. There is some question, according to Raymond Gariepy, that they might have owned a place at Saint Charles of Cape Tourmente from 1640 to 1646. (2)

Robert Gagnon, the fourth ancestor, arrived in 1655, and settled on a piece of land on the Ile d'Orleans; the said land was conceded to him the following year.

MATHURIN

He was born on 22 October 1606 at La Gagnonniere, two miles from Tourouvre where he was baptized. He lived there with his parents until he was 29 years old. He left for Canada in 1635 with his brothers. He opened a shop at Quebec: being the best educated, since he was the only one who could write, he kept the accounts. We note that he made a buying trip back to France in 1643 for their business. Toward 1640 he settled at Chateau-Richer on a grant of land 6.5 arpents in river frontage by 126 in depth: a survey in 1663 shows him located between the land of Michel Roullois and that of Pierre Gagnon, his brother. From 1646 to 1674, he bought and sold many pieces of land in Chateau-Richer. He even bought one of 16 January 1674, which he quickly turned over to his son Mathurin the following October 13th.

On 30 September 1647, when he was middle aged, he married Francoise Boudeau, daughter of Francois and of Jeanne Jehan or Panee, from Roche-Guyon in Normandy. Francoise's mother was previously married in France to Jacques Lehoux and they came to Canada together. Francoise was only thirteen years old when she married Mathurin while he was forty-one. The wedding took place in the home of Mathurin at Chateau-Richer. Jacques Lehoux signed as a witness to the marriage. (3)

They had sixteen children, but only nine lived to marry: 5 boys and 4 girls. Mathurin died and was buried on 20 April 1690 and Francoise on 14 September 1699 at Chateau-Richer.

JEAN

He was born on 13 August 1610 at the same place as Mathurin. On his arrival at Quebec in 1635, at age 25, he too went into the family business.

In 1640 he obtained a concession of 7 arpents in river frontage by 126 arpents deep, at Chateau-Richer. From 1640 to 1652 he too bought and sold land in Chateau-Richer, but he always kept that original grant received in 1640.

Jean married on 29 July 1640, at age 30, to Marguerite Cauchon, age 20, possibly at Chateau-Richer. She was the daughter of Jean and of Marguerite Cointal, originally from the town of Caux in the region of Dieppe in Normandy. Her mother died on 9 January 1633, then her father remarried on 4 April 1633 to Jeanne Abraham at Dieppe. Hence Marguerite, her brothers and sisters, came to Canada with their father and stepmother sometime after 1633.

Jean and Marguerite settled down on the arpents of land which had been conceded to them in 1640. A map of 1663 shows the place to measure 16 arpents to the east of Mathurin, between Jean Chapeleau and J. Lesot.

They had eight children: six were married, 2 boys and 4 girls, while 2 died at an early age. Jean was buried on 2 April 1670 at Chateau-Richer and as for Marguerite, no one is certain as to the date of her death or burial. (4)

PIERRE

This one was born on 14 February 1612 at la Gagnonniere and was baptized at Ventrouze, three miles from his birthplace. He was 23 years old when he came to Canada and went into business with his brothers.

Just as the other two, he obtained a concession at Chateau-Richer, between Mathurin his brother and Jean Cachon junior. His was a large grant of 6.5 arpents on the river by 126 arpents deep. On 13 May 1657, Pierre ceded a half arpent of his land to Nicolas Lebel, bordering that of Jean Cachon junior. He took it back on 29 December 1668.

When Jean was 30 years old, he cast his lot with that of Vincente Desvarieux, daugher of Jean and of Marie Chevalier of Saint Vincent of Aubermail, town of Caux, in Normandy. After their marriage on 14 September 1642 at Notre-Dame of Quebec, they settled in Chateau-Richer, where they had ten children. Two boys and a girl were married: Pierre-Paul was ordained a priest at Quebec in

1677 by Mgr de Laval. He was the first of his name and the third Canadian to become a priest. The other five children died at an early age.

One daughter of Pierre Gagnon entered the Convent of the Augustines at the age of 13 years. The Sisters of the Hospital of Quebec, at the death of Marie Madeleine, which happened in 1677 when she was only 22, wrote this about her: "Veritably, she was comparable to the angels in her purity, her obedience, her spirit of gentleness and peace, and for her devotion. . . ."

The burial of Vincente took place on 2 January 1695 and that of Pierre on 17 April 1699 at Chateau-Richer. (5)

The last Gagnon was born the 1st of March 1628 at Ventrouze, and was baptized in the same parish. He came to Canada in 1655 and obtained a land grant, of prime river frontage, on 2 April 1656, but it was only 4 arpents wide to a depth of about 64.5 arpents, up to where a road was going to be built. It was located between the property of Guillaume Landry and that of Jacques Perrot, at Saint-Famille on the Ile d'Orleans. According to the census of 1667, he had cleared 15 arpents and by 1681, 20 arpents were usable.

On 3 October 1657, at the age of 29 years, Robert married Marie Parenteau, age 16 years, Mgr De Queylus officiating. His dearly beloved was born in 1641, at Saint-Nicolas de la Rochelle. She had come to Canada as a "fille a marier": on the 1st of October 1657, during the forenoon, a contract of marriage signed by Notary Audouart was sent to her lodgings at a boarding house for young girls run by the Madames Bourdon and d'Aillebout. Marie said she was the daughter of Antoine Parenteau and of Anne Poisson. Her father was a carpenter and hewer of beams.

Robert and Marie settled down on the land he owned on the Ile d'Orleans. They had ten children: four boys and two girls married; two girls became nuns and two died at an early age.

They raised their entire family on the same farm where Robert died on 2 September 1703. As for Marie, having made her will on 19 October 1705 (Notary Chambelon), she died and was buried on 17 November that same year. Both repose in the cemetery of Sainte-Famille. (6)

The descendants of Robert, who all live on the south shore of the river Saint Lawrence, at Riviere Ouelle and at Rimouski, carry the surname Gagnon dit Belles-Iles or Gagnon dit Belzile.

Some claim that Robert was a cousin of the three brothers. Significantly, nothing in the marriage contracts of any of them indicates this. In France there was no apparent kinship between the two families. If they were relatives they were surely distant ones. The father and mother of Robert were the people who lived in the village of Ventrouze in Perche. These are the only details that we have on the subject.

Before finishing this, I have to tell you that Marguerite Gagnon, born 5 October 1598 at la Gagnonniere, sister of the three Gagnon brothers, also came to Canada. Marguerite was married at Ventrouze, France, on 3 February 1624 to Eloi Tavernier. After their marriage, they lived at Saint-Malo de Randonnai, from where Eloi came. They had at least two girls: Marguerite, born in 1627 and Marie in 1632, both at Saint-Malo, France.

In 1642 they sold their belongings in Saint-Malo and on the first of May 1644, they were in Quebec where their daughter Marguerite married Mace Gravel; he who was in business with the three Gagnons. Was it he who would come with Mathurin on his business trip to France in 1643?

One also finds at Chateau-Richer, in 1647, the mother Renee Roger witnessing the marriage contract of Mathurin. And some years later, it was no longer a question of her being here, but the question was would she return to France? Pierre, her husband, had already died in France, between the dates of 16 December 1630, when he signed for the death of his brother Olivier, and 1633 where, in a notarial act Renee Roger was called the widow of Pierre Gagnon.

A ROSE BY ANY OTHER NAME

In the various documents in France, at Tourouvre or at Ventrouze, one finds the following written: Gangnon, Gaignon, Gaingnon, Gasgnon or Gagnon. According to Dauzet, the sense of the name Gagnon could represent the mythical horned boar of Provence, or more likely in Normandy, a barnyard dog, nickname for a fierce man. The Gagnon family is one of the most numerous in French America. All of the Gagnons whom I know are excellent people! It is a Gagnon who tells you this!

In addition to the alternate surnames of Belzile and Belisle, some of the Gagnon descendants have taken the name Le Sauvage. (7)

BIBLIOGRAPHY

(1)	U	Volume I, pages 59 - 63
(2)	AG	The Seigneury of Beaupre
(3)	BQ	pages 15, 110, 113, 115, 127, 164
(4)	CZ	Volume I, pages 246 - 248. Volume IV, pages 135 - 137
(5)	BF	Volume 17, pages 302 - 211. Volume 34, pages 177 - 183
(6)	BM	Volume 19, pages 195 - 210
(7)	CZ	Volume 7, page 532

Vue de Québec – 1841

Antoine Lacasse

Chapter 12

Antoine Lacasse

*A*ntoine Casse dit Lacasse, was originally from Anjou, a French province serving as the gateway to Brittany, located between Maine and Poitou. He was baptized about 1641 at the Church of Saint-Pierre in Doue, today Doue-la-Fountaine, Department of Maine-et-Loire, District of Saumur. This church, with a very plain exterior, is remarkable for its three naves built during diverse epochs.

Antoine was the grandson of house-roofers Mathurin and Pierre Beaudoin. His father Noel, baptized at Doue the 1st of February 1619, married Michelle Durand about 1640. She gave him four children of whom Antoine was the eldest and Our Canadian Ancestor. (1)

TO THE COAST OF BEAUPRE

On Wednesday 14 October 1665 at Chateau-Richer, the Notary Claude Aubert prepared a contract of marriage between Antoine and his bride-to-be, Francoise Pitye. She was the daughter of Francois and of Claudine Poullet from the Parish of Saint Nicolas-du-Champs in Paris. Present at the signing were Romain Trepagner, Surgeon Francois Fortin and his wife Marie Jolliet, Charles Lefrancois and others. Because of an oversight, this contract was not entered in the records until the following March 28th, nevertheless the marriage took place the same day the contract was signed. Father Thomas Morel gave the nuptial benediction after having dispensed with the reading of the two banns. (2)

THE BEAUPRE COAST

On 16 June 1666, Antoine bought some property from Jean Baron, an associate of Mathurin Tessier. This land was 3 arpents of river frontage located at Saint-Pierre, Ile d'Orleans, between Robert Jeanne and Mathurin Chabot. It was formerly the land of Ancestor Savard and the price was 295 livres. Barthelemy Verreau was witness to this transaction. However, on 13 July 1667, Antoine signed it over to the brothers Adrian and Michel Isabel, before witnesses.

On 4 December 1666 Antoine broke a lease on a farm, a lease he had made with Antoine Berson, now dead. Berson's widow, Marguerite Belanger, accepted the cancellation and repossessed her property in the Fief of Lotinville, today the Ange-Guardian. She had to give him 215 livres in compensation and "a grey cloak that the said Casse vowed to have had and received from the master." She allowed him to keep the house and kitchen up until the next May; also a place in the shed to put "his part and portion of the grain." Such a compensation leads us to conclude that Antoine must have lived there for several years. The grey cloak—did it belong to the late Berson? Our man seemed to think so; no doubt it was made in France. (3)

David Letourneau, miller of the seigneury of Beaupre, but resident of the Ile d'Orleans, decided to sell his land to Lacasse. According to this deal, concluded on 15 August 1667, David vacated a property located on the south coast of the Island, next to that of Jean Letourneau and Jean Grignon, for the sum of 200 livres payable in two installments. The seller kept for himself only "those parts which are necessary for the grain milling process of said habitation" because they could be useful to his son Jean. After one year to the day, Jeanne Baril, his wife, ratified the sale. (4)

On Wednesday 2 November, Antoine would consent to assign "Jean Prevost of the city of Rouen come this present year to this country" to Jacques Ratte, resident of the Island. It seems that Antoine had agreed to take this immigrant for four years. And another matter, on 5 December Romain Trepanger admitted to owing Antoine 19 livres and 10 sols. (5)

Antoine, on 22 March 1669 still lived on the Beaupre coast. In order to pay the sum of 144 livres for merchandise received and delivered, Antoine agreed to pay back his creditor, Bertrand Chesnay, Seigneur of Lothainville, by Saint Michel's Day. He was to satisfy this debt "in money or in pelts;" was Antoine a beaver trapper? The witness to this notarial act was named Jean Casse. Could he have been a relative? There is nothing to indicate this: Jean Casse was 35 years old in 1667 and a former domestic of Charles Bazire. A Poitevan, he had married Magdeleine Plouard, a Breton, on 22 November 1667 at Chateau-Richer. This couple returned to France, after which we lose all trace of them. (6)

The 24th of the same month, Antoine asked Letourneau to accept 100 planks valued at 45 livres as a deduction from his debt. Robert Anest made these planks from pine wood and they were good and salable. He traded them to Lacasse for a fat pig. (7)

AT THE ILE d'ORLEANS

Antoine and Francoise settled down on the Island toward the end of 1669. It is a certainty that Lacasse lived on the Island on 14 February 1670, because from there he promised to deliver on the wharf at Quebec, with Pierre Dufresne, 500 planks to Jean B. Patoullet, for a price of 40 livres. (8)

The following April, Claude Charron, wealthy merchant of Quebec, sold a 5-year-old brown cow to Lacasse. The latter had to remit 18 livres-worth of salted butter in good condition in each of three years. If perchance, the poor beast had to give up her life because of the negligence of her adopted father, the latter was to pay half her value. He had to be poor in order to accept such conditions! (9)

Then follow several years of silence! On 18 January 1677 Lacasse sold his land on the south shore of the Island with all that was on it, to Pierre Bissonnet, for 500 livres. Up until the sale, Jean Letourneau and Francois Dumas were his neighbors. For the first time we discover the well-lettered signature of Our Ancestor next to that of Nicholas Gauvreau. The contract was made at Quebec by Pierre Duquet, notary. (10)

AT BEAUMONT

Our Ancestor was always attracted by the south. From the Beaupre coast he moved to the Island, into today's parish of Saint Laurent, then on to Beaumont. It was there, on 1 July 1698, where Father Thomas Morel baptized his daughter Charlotte.

In 1672, Charles Couillard had obtained the seigneury of Beaumont from Talon. According to the census of 1681, Antoine was one of fourteen colonists established on this territory. He owned a gun, 3 head of cattle and 8 arpents of cleared land. On the Beaupre coast in 1667 he had 3 beasts, 14 arpents of worthwhile land and a hired hand: he is not improving his position. (11) Did Antoine get his new bit of land on credit? Perhaps, because we note that he obtained the property of 4 arpents in frontage on 14 June 1682, but it was not until 1699 that it was officially conceded to him. (12)

In those times one went to Mass at Point Levy. For special occasions the manor house of the Seigneur served as a chapel. It was there on 9 August 1681, that Mgr de Lavel confirmed 7 people, among whom were Marie Casse, 17 years old, and her 12-year-old brother Joseph.

Lacasse owned, in company with Michel Mailloux-de-la-Durantaye, a beautiful boat complete with sails and ground tackle. Francois Frichet bought it on 18 July 1683 for the sum of 129 livres: he acted in the name of Pierre Lereau and Pierre Ducharme. (13)

In 1687 Pierre Bissonnet, now a farmer of Durantaye, left the land that he had bought from Casse, with the half arpent of frontage that he had added to it. Two years later, on 13 March 1689, Jean Jouanne bought it for 340 livres. (14)

LEAVING AND GIVING

On 28 March 1686, John Adam in the name of his Seigneur, conceded "three arpents of land in width and forty in depth" in order to enlarge the property of Antoine. The latter was not able to clear it, moreover he had to pay the seigneurial rents. Therefore, on 1 June 1699, he decided to abandon this concession. (15)

Antoine and Francoise, on 26 August 1702, had come to the end of their rope. "Desiring especially to spend the rest of their days in peace and tranquillity, in order to better care for their health," they made a donation to their son Charles. This heir became owner of 2 steers, 2 cows, one 14-year-old mare with her 4-month-old colt, and half of the coastal land to the northeast. In return, the son was expected to feed, house, clothe and to care for his parents until their death and afterward, to have 30 Requiem Masses said for the repose of their souls. At Quebec, the bailiff Etienne Maranda signed this donation as witness with Notary Chambelon.

THE FAMILY

This avalanche of detail should not cause you to forget that the family Lacasse worked a farm for survival. One feels that in this house there was hope for a better life—which never was realized.

The Lacasse parents had 9 children: 3 boys and 6 girls. Antoine the eldest baptized at Chateau-Richer in May of 1668, died at 19 in the flower of his youth. Joseph and Charles were the fruitful ones and perpetuated the name Lacasse in Canada and the USA.

Antoine left this world in 1709 and was buried at Beaumont the first day of June. Father Jean Pinguet wrote his death certificate at Lauzon. As for Francoise Pitie or Piloy, she died on 28 February 1713, at over 70 years of age, and was buried alongside her husband. She had been the godmother of the first child born at Beaumont; Francoise Mailloux, on 3 July 1679.

Joseph Lacasse worked on the construction of the first church at Beaumont; Charles was its first warden in 1711. The first Lacasse priest was born at Beaumont on 27 August 1785. His name was Joseph, son of Antoine and of Catherine Guay. He was Cure of Riviere-du-Loup, of Cacouna, of Ile-Verte and of Saint Henri-de-Lauzon. (16)

Such is the resume of the untalented life of this humble and hard-working ancestor, father of a dignified and numerous progeny.

Among their remarkable descendants, the presence of Pierre-Zacharie Lacasse (1845 - 1921) calls for attention. He was the son of a farmer, Joseph and of Marguerite Mirault of Saint-Jacques-de-l'Achigan. This Oblate of Mary Immaculate first exercised his missionary zeal among the Amerindians of Betsiamis. Then he preached many popular retreats for a dozen years. Following this, for a quarter-century, he devoted himself to the Manitoban Missions. His numerous activities however did not keep him from publishing a series of erudite works. He died at Gravelbourg, Province of Quebec. (17)

BIBLIOGRAPHY

(1) D   Father A.M. Parent, C.Cs.R.—Manuscript
(2) CB & F   14 November 1665, 16 June 1666, 4 December 1666, 13 July 1667, 24 March 1669
(3) AX   pages 58 - 59, 60 and 65
(4) CB & F   15 August 1667
(5) CB & F   2 November 1667
(6) CB & F   22 March 1669 and 23 November 1667
(7) CB & F   5 December 1667
(8) CB & K   14 February 1670
(9) CB & K   28 April 1671
(10) CB & Z   18 January 1677 and 19 April 1687
(11) AY   page 189
(12) CB & P   1 June 1699 and 26 August 1702
(13) CB & Z   18 July 1683
(14) CB & CD   13 March 1689
(15) CB & P   1 June 1699 and 26 August 1702
(16) CP   Volume I, page 313
      CR   page 46
(17) DA   page 405
      Y   page 224

Plan of Québec in 1660, by Jehan Bourdon (fragment).

fleuve St Laurent ou

1660-1662
PLACE ROYALE, Quebec
Residence of François and Françoise Lavergne

WEATHERS

François Lavergne

Chapter 13

Francois Lavergne

$\mathcal{F}$rancois Lavergne came from Limoges, at that time a city of sixteen churches. This humble pioneer had a spirit of adventure, courage and trust in God.

AT THE RIVER NICOLET

Francois first trod the soil of New France about 1670, where we find him working as a farmer at Nicolet. Most probably he obtained his concession by oral permission from Seigneur Arnould Loubias, a man held in high esteem by his tenants. (1)

In addition to clearing his land, this emigre from Limoges dreamed of building a home. In the fall of 1671, he went to Quebec in hopes of finding a companion. There he met the orphan Francoise Lefrancois, daughter of Anthoine and of Pasquette Renard of the Parish of Notre-Dame d'Ouville-la-Bientournee, in the Diocese of Lisieu. They thought so well of each other that on 12 October they went before Notary Romain Becquet to arrange a contract of marriage. It was done in the home of Madame Jean Bourdon, in the presence of the widow Anne Gasnier, the guardian of Francoise. Neighbors Nicolas Metru and Jean Baptiste Cosset completed the group. (2) The King added 50 livres as dowry to the wedding presents of the bride; this on top of the 300 livres she already brought to the union. The couple could not write but were able to give their word as bond. Francoise Lefrancois was most certainly one of those fine, strong and courageous girls, protected by the King of France. (3)

On the following 19th of October, the Vicar General of Quebec, Father Henri de Bernieres, blessed the marriage of Francoise Lefrancois and Francois Lavergne; he was 22 years old, a resident of the Riviere Nicolet, son of the late Francois and of Guillemette Peronne of Saint Michel-des-Lions, Limoges, France. The newlyweds spent their honeymoon aboard a boat enroute down the Saint Lawrence toward Nicolet, their new home.

THE FIRST HARVEST

If, in 1671, Quebec was a big village, Nicolet was an all-but-deserted place: about fifty colonists all told. Without a doubt, the couple found the winter long and monotonous. Life itself was no bed of roses, but finally spring broke through with its wild flowers; summer came bringing fresh vegetables and with the autumn came the harvest. On 13 September 1672 a son was given to them. A Recollet priest on a visit to Nicolet, Father Claude Moireau, baptized the baby on the 17th of the same month. Madame the godmother was Marie Toupin, wife of M. de Moras. The child got his first name, Arnoult, from his godfather, none other than the Seigneur himself; M. de Loubias, who had loaned the use of his house as a chapel. The baptism was registered in Trois-Rivieres. (4)

Notary Severin Ameau tells us that on 26 December 1672, Francois sold his land of 3 arpents of frontage and his house to Dominique Jutrat-dit-Desrosiers. M. de Loubias had also quit the place to return to France, never to return. (5)

Early in 1673, the Lavergne family was living at Quebec. Francoise was reunited with Madame Bourdon, Father de Bernieres and her other friends. The family lived in the lower town, as we gather from the baptismal certificates of their children. Five more children came into the world: Marie-Anne, baptized on 19 November 1673, was a gift on the second anniversary of their marriage. Then came Joseph and Jeanne and the baptism of the youngest, Helene, on 3 September 1681, where we learn that Francois

Lavergne also called himself a mason. The records of the Seminary of Quebec give us the assurance that Francois worked, from 21 November 1677 to 8 April 1682, on the construction of this Seminary of Mgr de Laval. This big job, lasting from 1674 to 1683, employed many workers, among whom we find the carpenter Robert Levesque. The second book of accounts has a line which tells us the salary of Francois: "Fifty ecus and a pair of shoes." (6)

FRANCOISE AND THE SOVEREIGN COUNCIL

Monday, 26 August 1675, Francoise Lefrancois "wife of Francois Lavergne" in company with Marguerite Brassard, wife of the joiner Jean Lesmelin, came before the Sovereign Council as witnesses on the subject of a dispute that took place between the plaintiff Robert Mossion and the defendant Charles Marquis. The latter had struck "a pregnant sow with a kick in her behind that turned her over on her back with feet reaching heavenward, a situation from which she died due to her condition." Francoise swore under oath "that she lived in the house of Jean Dubuc, and that she heard the sow squeal at least three times while being kicked. She was able to hear this commotion because she was in the foyer nearby the door." It is not necessary to add that the aggressor was found guilty and sentenced to pay damages. (7)

FRANCOIS BECOMES A FARMER

In the space of about twenty-five years Francois Lavergne made at least five leases, concluded 5 or 6 business deals and honored several commissions as a stonemason, one of which was for the Ursulines of Quebec.

On the 25th of August 1683, Jean-Baptiste Morin de Rochebelle, a merchant of Quebec, sold a building to Francois that measured 45 feet in frontage by 100 feet in depth "alongside the Mount Carmel Road" in the upper city. The price was 100 sols of annual rent. But on 5 November 1685, in the presence of the same notary, Francois sold it back to Rochebelle with "an apartment and some rooms below" for the sum of 60 livres. (8)

FRANCOIS THE FARMER

Ever since practicing his trade of mason Francois had been looking for his own home. On 2 April 1691, Paul Dupuy, Royal Attorney to the Provost of Quebec, leased to Francois "title to the farm and its harvest of grain" for 5 years. The deal included the manor house on his Fief at l'Ile-aux-Oies, with all that goes with it. Arnoud Lavergne the son, who had been farming that same plot since he was ten years old, went in with his father to make it prosper. The conditions of the contract, forcefully spelled out in detail, seemed to favor the Lavergne family. Was it because Francois had difficulty coming up with the 90 minots of wheat that first year? Or did the requirement to provide the lessor with 20 pounds of good butter for each cow on the aforesaid farm, not to mention "the barrels of salt pork in good condition," finally discourage him? (9) Perhaps too, it may have been that the son had a lot more experience and tenacity than the father. In any event, the boy took to wife one Marguerite Daniau-Dancause on 25 March 1694, while the father gave up the lease and turned the entire operation over to his son.

It was during this period that the first death in the family occurred. On 12 March 1692, their third child, the sixteen year old Francois, was buried. The act was recorded at Cape Saint Ignace. (10)

BACK TO THE FARM

In 1694 Francois left "Goose Island" for the south shore. He accepted a verbal concession from Jean-Baptiste Couillard de Lespinay, but he abandoned it the same autumn. At the end of October Our Ancestor is mentioned by the Notary Chambelon as being in debt to Pierre du Roy of Quebec. He was known as a farmer of the Riviere-du-Sud, that is to say of Saint-Pierre de Montmagny.(11)

JOYS AND SORROWS

On 10 June 1699, Madame Lavergne was buried at Quebec at the age of about 50 years. Father Francois Dupre added the following to the notation of burial, "after having received the Sacraments of Penance, the Viaticum and Extreme Unction."

On 19 September 1702 at Quebec, Francois married again to Jeanne Chartier, widow of Pierre Roussel. But six years later she too died, probably at Saint-Pierre-du-Sud, in 1708. Her funeral took place on 31 December and the notation is recorded at Montmagny.

The following year on 15 April, Francois married for the third time to Renee Birette, widow of Jean Brais and of Pierre Balan dit Lacombe, before the Cure of Beaumont; act recorded at Saint-Michel. After a few years of happiness, it was Francois turn to be called to heaven. On 27 June 1714, at the age of about 72 years, "after having received the Holy Sacraments of Penance, the Viaticum and Extreme Unction, the next day he was buried in the cemetery of the Church of Saint Michel de Ladurantaye." Father Louis Mercier, ordained after the 1st of October 1713, Cure of Beaumont, registered the act at Beaumont, along with that of Renee Birette who died on 14 March 1715. Father Mercier himself died at the age of 29 years on 7 May 1715. (12)

POSTHUMOUS GLORIES

It seems that Francois Lavergne must have spent his entire life chasing rainbows. The farmers vocation was surely not his calling, but was masonry to his liking, or merely a way of putting bread on the table for his family?

Arnault, his only son, perpetuated the family name; he was also known as Rene, Arnaud and Renaud. His descendants are especially distinguished in the liberal arts professions where the spirit of words is greater than the force of arms. The Honorable Joseph Lavergne, lawyer, opened his office at Princeville in 1872. In 1874 he formed a legal society at Arthabaska. Named Judge of the Superior Court for the District of Ottawa in 1897, he was transferred ten years later to the Judicial District of Montreal. (13)

Armand Lavergne, the best known of all, was a jingoistic political orator quite capable of bringing his audience out of their seats, or to impale a reluctant adversary with a succinct phrase. Armand began his brilliant career at the age of 24 years as a Deputy from Montmagny.

The descendants of Our Ancestor Francois Lavergne took many family names: Boui, Bouis, Bouy, Boyou, Comparion, Comperon, Lebuy, Renauld, Sauviot, Tefe-Laguerche and Tetrau. (14)

BIBLIOGRAPHY

(1)	L	pages 44 - 45 and 49 - 50
(2)	CB & K	12 October 1671
(3)	Y	pages 227 - 228
(4)	AY.1	Volume 2, page 306
(5)	CB & B	26 December 1672
(6)	E	C.-L., page 404
(7)	BT	Volume I, pages 981 - 982
(8)	CB & AH	25 August 1683, 5 November 1685
(9)	CB & AH	2 April 1691
(10)	CZ	Volume I, page 355
(11)	CB & P	10 October 1694, 30 October 1694, 23 April 1703
(12)	CR	History of Beaumont
(13)	BF	Volume 35, page 99 and Volume 39, pages 422 - 423
(14)	CZ	page 555
	W	Volume III, page 174
	CT	pages 304-305
	CX	Volume V, page 57 col. b
		page 78 col. b
	BG	Volume 18, pages 157 - 170
	CJ	Volume 16, page 42;
		Volume 17, pages 40, 48, 53 and 54

Nicolas Leroy

Chapter 14

Nicolas Leroy

$\mathcal{N}$icolas Leroy, son of Louis and of Anne Le Mestre, was baptized at Saint-Remy de Dieppe, Normandy, the 25th of May 1639. He married Jeanne Lelievre while still very young and on 26 November 1658, their son Louis was baptized at Saint-Remy. (1)

A FAMILY ON THE MOVE

Why did Nicholas Leroy came to Canada? Was it because his father was dead and he had to support his mother? His father-in-law, Guillaume Lelievre, widower, went to New France sometime after 1656. The good word that he sent back invited Nicolas to emigrate, so together, the family decided to move to a new country. There were five of them in all: Nicolas, his wife, his mother, son Louis and baby Nicolas. (2)

We are able to fix precisely the date of arrival of this family in New France because of the following document taken from the Archives of France: "On Friday the 17th of June 1661, before Michel Manichet, Royal Notary in the Vicomte of Arques, and Antoine Le Marchal, Notary of Dieppe was present Nicolas Leroy, citizen of Dieppe, who promises by these presents to pay or to have paid to the Honorable Jean Gloria, merchant of the said Dieppe, a loan made in order to voyage to Canada, in the ship commanded by Captain Poullet of this city. Eight days after his arrival at the said place, will be paid the sum of fifty livres for the passage by the said Le Roy, who admits to have received payment from the said Gloria. If there should be any delay or refusal of said payment in the amount at the time aforesaid, the said Gloria may dispose of the matter as he may best see fit. Made and done, to which the said Le Roy pledges himself and his belongings, in the presence of Guillaume Loy and Jacques Ledoyen, of said Dieppe, Loy, with initials, J. Gloria; Nicollas Leroy." (3)

The reader of this authentic text is led to believe that the Leroys left their homeland in June 1661. The genealogist Michel Langlois has confirmed this from the Journal of the Jesuits: "Nicolas Le Roy arrived in the country on 22 August 1661 aboard the ship of Laurent Poullet." (4)

At Quebec, Nicolas, his wife Jeanne Lelievre, his mother, and their children, were warmly received by Guillaume Lelievre, who was already well acclimated to the region. He had remarried in 1660 to the widow Marguerite Millet; it was a grand reunion for the two families now united in Canada.

THE FAMILY SETTLES DOWN

Nicolas did not lose any time finding work to his liking in the Seigneury of Beaupre. On 6 October 1663 Nicolas received a concession from Guillemette Hebert, the widow Couillard. The same year, Grandmother Leroy, Anne Le Mestre, married Adrien Blanquet, a weaver by trade. And on 8 June 1664, in the presence of Notary Duquet, Nicolas officially acquired his land of two arpents in width by a mile in depth, to the east of the falls of Montmorency, today called Boischatel. (5) A cabin was built and the Leroy family lived on this farm perhaps up until 1679, the date of the sale of the two arpent property, one to Jacques Martelle, the other to Rene Brisson. (6)

They had added to the family with the following births: Noel, Marie, Guillaume, Jean, Marie-Elizabeth and Jean Baptiste the youngest, age one year. (7)

Nicolas had conquered the land. The census of 1666 mentions the name of Jean Briere, his farmhand. Nicolas also had an employee who made money for him; a sort of fish-warden. It's not just today that Canadians are poachers! In 1667 Nicolas owned 4 animals and 7 arpents of workable land. (8)

SOME SHOCKING EVENTS

If ever there was a couple who did not give trouble to others it was Nicolas Leroy and his wife. But one day, against his heart, he had to seek recourse in justice. It was in 1669.

A single man by the name of Jacques Nourry lived in the region from about the fall of 1651. He came from Feings in France and was known there as Pierre Maheux. In 1660 Charles Legardeur of Tilly leased him a place in the suburbs of Quebec for five years. Then in 1664, Jacques acquired a property measuring 2 arpents in frontage not far from the Montmorency cataract on the Beaupre coast. His neighbor was Charles Garnier. (9) The farm of Nourry and that of Leroy were about fifteen arpents apart. The census of 1667 tells us that Jacques Nourry, age 29 years, had 6 arpents under cultivation. One day in the summer of 1669, Mr. Jacques Nourry encountered the little 5-year-old daughter of Nicolas and Jeanne. Nourry violated Marie, but the matter did not stop there.

On 9 August the Leroy parents, deeply hurt, swore out a warrant in the name of the girl. Three doctors gave their opinion during a confrontation between the violator and the victim. The next day the Assistant Attorney General gave his summary to the Sovereign Council. The 12th day of the same month, exemplary justice dictated:

> "The Sovereign Council has decided and does declare that the said Jacques Nourry is guilty of the act and convicts him of having violated the said Marie Leroy and in reparation does condemn him to be hanged and strangled on a gallows; then his body taken to a public place where his head shall be severed and placed on a post—this to give thought to those who would avoid marriage. Three

hundred livres in civil damages to be given to the said Marie Roy, another one hundred livres in damages; a third to go to the hospital and two thirds to the Council for court costs. The remainder of his estate to be confiscated by the Lord of the High Court of Beaupre. Made and done by the Court at Quebec the 12th of August 1669."

On 7 September the authorities awarded the farm of Nourry to Charles Garnier. As for Marie Leroy, baptized at Quebec on 15 August 1664, the goddaughter of Michele Nau, wife of Sieur Joseph Giffard the Marquis of Beauport, she grew up quite normally. She became the wife of Jean Gaudreau on 31 July 1679, was the mother of 3 children and lived at Cape Saint Ignace.

ON THE SOUTH SHORE

Some events that happen in the life of a family cause a loathing for the environment surrounding the circumstances. Thus it seems, the Leroys were searching for an occasion to change location. On 13 August 1676, Nicolas Leroy was godfather to Anne Catherine Moleur dit Lallemand, at La Durantaye. Good-bye to the Beaupre coast, the friends, the neighbors! Nicolas and Jeanne with 7 children took to the river and canoed around the Ile d'Orleans in the direction of the vast domain of the Seigneur Oliver Morel a la Durantaie, within the boundaries of Beaumont. The 1st of August 1681, he and his wife were confirmed by Mgr de Laval. The first year there, this colonist owned 8 animals, 20 arpents of usable land and a gun. His two elder sons had their own land alongside their father. Inevitably, one after another the children left the nest as the other side of life approached.

Nicolas died between April 1690 and October 1691. As for Jeanne Lelievre, she married for a second time on 8 February 1695 to Francois Molinet, whose origins remain a mystery. Jeanne lived on for a number of years and was buried on 11 January 1728 at Saint-Vallier.

Many descendants of Nicolas have brought honor to Church and Country. The spirit of work and of research seems to characterize the honorable and grand family Roy. For example, we may cite Mgr Paul-Eugene Roy, Archbishop of Quebec, founder of the journal L'Action; and Pierre-Georges Roy, one of the most remarkable archivists of the Province of Quebec. The Cardinal Maurice Roy, Archbishop of Quebec, Primate of the Church of Canada, is also a descendant of Our Ancestor Nicolas Leroy.

Some descendants of Nicolas Leroy used the surname Lert, and others adopted the name Roy.

From the family name Roy, the following thirty (30) names devolved: Audy, Chatellereau, Dagenais, De la Barre, De la Potherie, DeMarau, De Monte-a-Peine, Desjardins, De St. Lambert, Duroy, La Cerene, LaLiberte, Lapensee, Larose, Lasseigne, Lauzier, Lepage, LeRoy, L'Eveille, Libois, Louvois, Poitevin, Portelance, Portelas, Roiroux, Royhart, Sauvage, St. Amour, St. Louis, and Tintamarre. (10)

BIBLIOGRAPHY

(1) AKI   pages 67 - 68
(2) CO1   255 pages
(3) BF   1929, page 697
(4) AV   Volume 2, page 397
(5) AG   page 115
(6) CB & Z   14 April 1677 and 30 March 1679
(7) CZ   Volume 1, page 532
(8) CE   Le Premier Recensement de la Nouvelle-France 1666:
               Volume 1, page 54
(9) CB & Z   1 January 1664
(10) CZ   Volume 7, pages 560 and 587
      AB   la Revue Populaire, Vol. 26, March 1949, page 2
      BV1   No. 14, 3 pages
      CX   Volume IV, page 54 col. b; page 73 col. b;
               Volume V, page 77 col. a
      CX1   Volume XIV, page 167

Etienne Lessard

Chapter 15

Etienne Lessard
by Renald Lessard

*É*tienne de Lessard, son of Jacques and of Marie Herson, was originally from Chambois in Normandy. In 1645, at about the age of 22, he left for New France, a distant colony of a few hundred harassed people. On 3 June 1646 we pick up his trail at Trois-Rivieres where he was acting as a godfather. For a period of several years Etienne was associated with Martin Grouvel, a river pilot of Quebec. It is probably this association that accounts for his presence in 1646-47 at Trois-Rivieres and at Tadoussac. (1)

HIS MARRIAGE

On 8 April 1652 at Quebec, Etienne de Lessard and Marguerite Sevestre were betrothed. She was the daughter of Charles, a notable of Quebec, and their union was "in the presence of the recognized witnesses Mr. de Lauson Gouverneur, Mr. de Lauson junior, Fils Seneschal, and Mr Chartier." The couple installed themselves at Sainte-Anne-de-Beaupre. (2)

COLONIST AT SAINTE ANNE

In reality, Etienne had already obtained a concession on the spot from Olivier Letardif, one of the members of the Beaupre Company; which concession was granted him on 10 February 1651. It comprised 10 arpents of river front-age, extending to a depth of a league and a half inland. In order to clear his land, named Saint Etienne, he had a few indentured workers in his service; such as Michel Marquiseau, Urbain Jamineau and Jean Chauvet dit Lagerne. By 1669 they had already cleared 35 arpents and, according to the census of 1681, Lessard said that he owned 3 guns, 7 head of cattle, and 40 arpents of cleared land. On this land he grew—among other things—wheat, barley, peas and even some cabbage. (3)

COMMERCE AND NAVIGATION

Etienne was a very active man. He carried on business relations with many merchants such as Charles Aubert, Sieur de la Chesnaie de Quebec and Daniel Baille, Sieur de Saint-Meur de La Rochelle in France. Lessard owned a boat, a rather large one considering the times, about 30 by 13 feet. It had a cabin at either end which made it seem elegant indeed and was configured to carry cargo, often between Quebec and Sainte-Anne. Be this as it may, his principal occupation seems to have been cultivating the land. (4)

A SEIGNEUR

Etienne was the first Seigneur of the Ile-aux-Coudres. In fact, this seigneury was conceded to him by Frontenac on 4 March 1677. Lessard sold it to the Seminary of Quebec in 1687 for 100 livres. On 27 April 1688 he became co-seigneur of Lanoraie, a domain situated between Trois-Rivieres and Montreal. He sold his part on 12 March 1698 to Jean Bredel before the Notary Charles Rogeot. (5)

THE FIRST CHURCH AT BEAUPRE—1658

In 1658, Saint-Anne-de-Beaupre was called Petit Cap (The Little Cape), and the little settlement already counted about twenty families. The land-grant lists and records of the Seigneury of Beaupre, still preserved in the Quebec Seminary, make it possible for us to reconstitute the Petit Cap as it then was.

On March 8 of that year, in an official deed drawn up by the royal Notary Audouart, Etienne de Lessard "seeing the inclination and devotion that the settlers of Beaupre have long had to have a church or chapel in which they might assist at Divine Service and participate in the Sacrements of Our Holy Mother the Church, donates a lot of two arpents wide, by a league and half deep, to the Pastors who will be established there. The said donation being made on condition that in the present year of 1658 work be begun and continued without let-up for the building of a church or chapel by the inhabitants of the place, on the said lot, at the place which will be decided upon as most handy, in the opinion of the Vicar General." (6)

There was no delay. On the following March 13, Father Jean de Quen, S.J. could note in the Jesuit Diary, that "the acting Governor (Monsieur d'Ailleboust), went that day to the Beaupre shore to see if work was being carried out on the small forts that served for their protection. The Reverend Father Vignal blessed the site of the new church. My Lord the Governor laid the first stone thereof." (7)

It is still possible, today, to identify with some precision the site of this first church of 1658, situated on the river shore at the high-water line, according to a report made in 1686, addressed to Father de Maizerets and still extant in the Quebec Seminary's archives. (8)

Little is known of the building of the 1658 church. On December 10, 1659, in the presence of Father LeMercier, Mr. Jean Picard, Warden of the Church of St. Anne of the Petit Cap, presented a financial report. The Church still owed him, for his work, thirty-four livres and ten sols. (9) On March 18, 1660, Nicolas Verieul made a donation to the church of St. Anne of the Petit Cap "to help out on the building." The church is said to be "already begun." (10) The church of 1658 was set on an elevated spot near the shore. In the choice of this site, little account had been taken of the spring high tides, particularly those which occur every seven years. The note addressed to Father de Maizerets on July 7, 1686 clearly states: "The church of Saint Anne was for the first time placed at high tide level on the river shore, and then moved higher to the foot of the bluff, on account of the inconvenience of the waters that surrounded it at its first site." (11) The decision had to be made, then, to transport the chapel, or to build a new one, further away from the shoreline, and especially higher up than the high water mark. It was not possible to build elsewhere, on ground donated by Etienne de Lessard on March 8, 1658, for there was not enough room between the bluff and the river shore.

THE CHURCH OF 1661

Urged by his own generosity, and also, perhaps, by the desire to keep the church on his grant of land, Etienne de Lessard made a verbal offer of an adjacent plot of land to the east of the original grant. Bishop Laval gladly accepted, for on that particular spot, the ground rose to about ten feet above sea level, and the hillside retreats landwards for about fifty feet. If the church was built parallel to the river, then there would be lots of space.

It was built in record time. (12) First, Robert Pare and Jean Picard dragged the wood to the spot, using Etienne Lessard's oxen which had been lent for four days. Then Jean Picard sawed out the chevrons and measured off the planks. Less than three weeks after, a pot of vine was given to a person named Bontemps, and identified as Francois Boivin, in exhange for the first wooden peg set in the building. (Wooden pegs were more often used than the hard-to-come-by iron nails.)

The edifice was to be forty feet long. Instead of making the walls by laying one beam on top of the other, then the most usual procedure, they were built in what is known as "colombage pierrotte" (half-timbers). This method consisted of laying a field-stone foundation, on which a cedar frame was laid. Into this were mortised four-by-eight upright beams, at regular distances of about one foot. The intervening spaces were then filled with stones and mortar. We know that Louis Cauchon, of Chateau-Richer, sold for this purpose twelve "pipes" (hogsheads) of lime. Jean Picard took five days to float it to the building site, using Etienne Lessard's boats.

Two craftsmen who boarded in the homes of Lessard and of Pierre Giguere worked for a whole month with the master mason, Pierre Simard, nicknamed Lombrette, on the exterior of the church. Father Ragueneau, S.J. on one of his visits from Quebec to see how the work was coming along and to encourage the workers, brought with him the roofing nails. We can conclude, then, that the outside of the church was finished when Father Thomas Morel arrived from France, on August 22, 1661, to be almost at once named by Bishop Laval for the ministry along the Beaupre Shores. (13)

THE DEATH OF MARIE PICHON

On the death, in February, 1662, of Marie Pichon, widow of Charles Sevestre, Etienne inherited a "half of a cellar, half of a hayloft, some rooms serving as a bakery and a fourth of the courtyard, altogether consisting of a fourth part of the house and courtyard belonging to the late Master Charles Sevestre, formerly Lieutenant of this jurisdiction (Quebec), the said house situated in the lower town, Rue Notre-Dame. (14) Many times he rented out his part of the house and finally on 6 April 1683 he sold it to Francois Hazeur and Etienne Lander on "That remainder which may be useful, together with everything inside that is left after the fire of the 4th and 5th of last August." (15)

THE DONATION

On 26 March 1699, Marguerite and Etienne, "being victims of their old age, which is advanced and renders them infirm and subject to the natural indisposition which accompanies the aged, and which causes a loss of spirit and force, they find themselves no longer able to handle their own affairs and it is of more advantage to them now to give or to sell their heritage to their two children named Prisque and Joseph." As for the children, "they will feed and care for their father and mother and treat them according to their station in life. Their rooms shall be clean and heated so as to stave off illness for the remainder of their days and at the end of their time, they shall be buried, and prayers shall be offered for the repose of their soul, according to the customs." Etienne was 66 years old when this act was made. (16)

HIS DEATH

The month of April 1703 was a time of bereavement for the Lessard family, because on the 21st, Etienne was buried "dead at the age of 80 years, on the day before about 3 in the afternoon, after having received all the Sacraments and after having given all the thoughts and sentiments of a good Christian and true Child of the Church." Etienne was probably a victim of the smallpox epidemic then sweeping the colony. His wife Marguerite survived him for 17 more years. (17)

HIS DESCENDANTS

Eleven children were born from his union with Marguerite Sevestre, of whom 6 boys and 2 girls were later married. The descendants of Etienne de Lessard are dispersed throughout the Province, but they are particularly numerous in the region of Quebec City and the Beauce. Some adoped the name DeLessard and a few even LaToupie. (18) Let us note in conclusion that Etienne was a respected man in spite of some problems with the law. He was a Captain of Militia (1684) and also Warden of Sainte-Anne. (19)

BIBLIOGRAPHY

(1)	CG	3 June 1646 and 16 April 1647
(2)	CH	8 April 1652
(3)	CA	MG1, G1, Vol. 460.1 page 38
		MG1, G1, Vol. 460.2 page 161
		MG1, G1, Vol. 460.3 page 352
(4)	Q	Alludes to the boat of Lessard.
(5)	CB	Rageot, Charles. 12 March 1698
(6)	CB & H	8 March 1658
(7)	AV	pages 232 - 233
(8)	C1	7 July 1686
(9)	D	Account Book, Volume 1, sheet 1, recto.
(10)	CB & F	18 March 1660
(11)	CI	7 July 1686
(12)	D	Account Book, Volume 1, Sheet 2.
(13)	AF1	pages 6, 7, 8, 9 and 27
(14)	CB & AL	4 February 1662
(15)	CB & CD	6 April 1683
(16)	CB & AS	24 March 1699, la donation
(17)	CI	21 April 1703
(18)	CZ	page 560
(19)	CI	4 April 1684
	CB & H	19 February 1652, 3 May 1653, 26 October 1653, 24 July 1657, 14 May 1658, 23 July 1658 and 6 August 1660
	CB & F	27 January 1659 and 3 March 1692
	CB & K	14 September 1669, 15 November 1669, 20 March 1670, 19 August 1670, 30 September 1670, and 23 August 1673
	CB & CD	30 January 1672, 17 August 1676, 19 December 1679, 10 October 1681, 11 July 1685 and 27 July 1688
	CB & AH	9 February 1684 and 19 October 1687
	CB & AS	29 July 1698 and 22 June 1704
	CB & P	27 February 1700 and 18 June 1704
	AQ	23 October 1668
	E	Paroisses diverses No. 73, 75. Documents Faribault 78 Procure, Carton Sainte-Anne, 15 Seminaire 35, No. 43
	CU	pages 79, 182 - 183, 204 - 205, 227, 235
	AV	pages 89 and 100
	BT	pages 785 - 786 and 797
	CE	page 173s

Robert Lévesque

Chapter 16

Robert Levesque

$\mathscr{R}$obert Levesque, son of Pierre and Marie Caumont, was baptized about 1641. He was originally from the town of Hautot-Saint-Sulpice, Department of the Seine-Inferieure, Arrondissement of Yvetot, Canton of Doudeville, Province of Normandy, France.

ROBERT SETTLES IN FRANCE

Why did Robert come to Canada when he was already almost thirty years old? It's a mystery! It seems probable but by no means certain, that he arrived in New France in June of 1671. He was thought to have been aboard the ship SAINT JEAN BAPTISTE, in company with J.B. Francois Deschamps, the future Seigneur de la Boutelliere. They were accompanied by "two carpenters, two masons, and four laborers," whose job it would be to clear up to 1000 arpents of the land given to Deschamps as a grant from the King. One of these carpenters was Our Ancestor Robert Levesque.

Seigneur Deschamps, considering discretion the better part of valor, abandoned this concession from the King because of the Iroquois menace. He obtained another in a more hospitable area from Jean Talon, the King's Intendant, on 29 October, 1672. It was to become the settlement known as Riviere-Ouelle. One can imagine the bustle of activity as laborers, masons, carpenters and all hands turned to erecting shelters before winter set in.

The name of Robert Levesque is mentioned officially for the first time on 10 November 1674. This was the day he received his own grant of land from his Seigneur. (3) It read: "containing 12 arpents of frontage on the river Ouelle and

30 in depth, of uninhabited land in the said seigneury". Moreover, "given and conceded 3 arpents of frontage by 6 in depth in the grasslands to the south, called The Grand Anse, with the right to fish salmon at the spot called the Point of the Southwest". We know also that after this date Robert worked as a carpenter on building the Seminary of Quebec. (4).

On 22 April 1679, at l'Ange-Gardien, Robert married Jeanne Le Chevalier. Of course this was preceded by a contract of marriage, written up by Notary Paul Vachon the day before. Jeanne was about 34 years old, the daughter of Jean and of Marguerite Romain of Saint-Nicolas de Cou-stances, in The Manche, Normandy. (6) A young Canadian missionary priest, Guillaume Gaultier, himself born at Quebec in 1653, blessed the marriage. Mathurin Huot and Charles Letartre assisted at the wedding as witnesses.

This was the second marriage for Jeanne Le Chevalier. She was the widow of Guillaume Lecanteur, Sieur de la Tour, son of Nicolas and of Jeanne Hamelot of Saint-Sauvier de Beaumont-en-Auge, Normandy. Lecanteur was already living in Quebec as early as 9 July 1670. He signed his marriage contract with Jeanne on 11 October 1671. (7) This couple lived in the Ange-Gardien near Quebec. There they had three children: Nicolas, Charles and Guillaume. When the census of 1681 was taken, Nicolas and Charles were mentioned but not Guillaume. Then Charles disappeared too. (8) Years later, on 24 September 1693, Robert Levesque gave his remaining step-son a piece of property of 6 arpents in frontage on the river Ouelle. Sometime between that date and 4 October 1693, a period of about two weeks, Nicolas died., We know because that was the date on which his mother Jeanne had the gift annulled because her son was dead. (9)

A BIG LANDOWNER

While Robert Levesque lived at Riviere-Ouelle he was known as a carpenter, but he made more of a living out of farming and the land. According to the census of 1681, Robert owned 4 guns, 11 head of cattle, and 10 arpents of land under cultivation. On 20 June 1683 Robert acquired another property. (10) Then, in one single deal with Joseph Renaud and his wife Marie Lehoux, on 11 August 1692, Robert bought three parcels of land and a house on the river Ouelle, in what must have been one of the most complicated land transactions of the time. As best can be deciphered from the none too distinct text, it went something like this:

"One piece measuring 12 arpents in frontage by 42 in depth, is adjoined to the southeast by lands not yet conceded, and on the other side by the property of Rene Hoylet in part, and by that of the seller . . .plus a beautiful large parcel of farm land located between the land already specified above, and that of Damien Berube, who lives to the southwest; to the unassigned lands bordered on two sides by the river Ouelle . . . the remainder of the six arpents of land conceded by Deschamps to Pierre Michel on 18 May 1683, having been conceded after the other part of the land of the aforesaid six arpents, to Rene Ouelet . . . plus half a point of land . . . opposite to the holdings of Pierre Hudon, that of the heirs of the late Jacques Miville and Pierre Dancosse, following the act of concession of the seller, made on 30 July last (1692), in order to replace and compensate for the part subtracted from the six arpents above . . ." Whatever it may have said, one thing is clear: Robert Levesque became about as big a landholder as existed at the time.(11)

A PATRIOT

In 1690, the British Admiral Sir William Phipps, tried to take Quebec. En route, he menaced the settlements along the Saint Lawrence. His fleet made an attempt to disembark troops at Riviere-Ouelle. The Reverend Pierre Terrier of Francheville, a fiery but provident patriot, Cure of Rivere-Ouelle from 1689 to 1692, organized the defense. A dozen men hid in the underbrush along the bank and there we find Robert Levesque, weapon in hand. They waited until the soldiers were in boats and approaching the shore before opening fire. The surprised Englishmen retreated back to the tending ship, POINTE, and sailed away. At least Riviere-Ouelle was saved for awhile. (12)

HIS DESCENDENTS

Robert Levesque was buried at Riviere-Ouelle on 13 September 1699. The Cure De Roqueleyne wrote in the register that Robert had died "The 11th of the current month." Assisting at his interment we find Guillaume Lisot and Robert Morin. Our ancestor was about 58 years old and father of 6 children: 5 boys and a girl Marie-Anne, who died a short time after she was born on 15 October 1690. Today his descendents are numerous throughout North America; especially in Quebec, in the Maritime Provinces and in New England. Many politicians, businessmen, priests, brothers, nuns, and even a few bishops have come from the direct line of Robert Levesque. (13)

A THIRD MARRIAGE

After the death of her second husband, on 15 April 1701 Jeanne Le Chevalier married the first Seigneur of the Riviere-Ouelle, none other than Jean-Baptiste Francois Deschamps himself.

Deschamps was baptized in 1646 at Cliponville, a town in the Department of the Seine-Inferieure, Arrondissement of Yvetot, in Normandy. He was the son of Jean and of Elizabeth Debin. He was a dignified man, very preoccupied with the welfare of his family and his tenants, who honored him. He spent 50,000 livres of his own money to develop his seigneury. His first marriage was to Catherine-Gertrude Macard on 24 October 1672, at Quebec. Their contract of marriage was made before Notary Romain Becquet on the 16th of the same month. Gertrude was the daughter of Nicolas and of Marguerite Couillard. J.B. Francois and Gertrude had 5 children between 1673 and 1681: Charles-Joseph Deschamps became a priest; J. Francois was baptized at the Riviere-Ouelle on 20 September 1681 and died at an early age; Louis-Henri, husband of Louise-Genevieve De Ramzay, was appointed as Aide-Major at Quebec, as a Captain in the Marine Corps, and as Commandant at Detroit.

Gertrude Macard was buried on 21 November 1681. We find her burial record at l'Islet since the parish of Riviere-

Ouelle was not yet organized. The first baptism written in the parish record of Riviere-Ouelle, by Father Pierre Permelnaud, and dated 6 January 1685, was that of Joseph Levesque, son of Robert and Jeanne. It was after 20 years as a widower, therefore, that the Seigneur Deschamps married Jeanne on 15 April 1701. But he too was buried in his turn on 16 December 1703 at Riviere-Ouelle.

As for Jeanne Le Chevalier, she lived on for several more years. Father Bernard De Roqueleyne celebrated her funeral Mass on 25 November 1716. He wrote in the register "Dame Jeanne Chevaillier wife of the late monsieur Deschamps de la Bouteeillerie (and widow of Robert Levesque) died the 24th of the current month with the sacraments of the church at age of about 78 years. Assisting at her burial were Jacque Boy and Jacque Gagnon who have signed." (15)

Some descendents of our ancestor Robert Levesque have taken the names of Leveque and Sansoucy. (15)

BIBLIOGRAPHY

(1) BF   Volume 15, page 123
(2) AP   Pages 462 and 16, 33, 39
(3) CB & K   10 November 1674
(4) CJ   Volume XVI, page 42
(5) CB & DK   21 April 1679
(6) X   In place of Romain, this source has transcribed Scorban or Scorman.
(7) CB & K   11 October 1671
(8) AY   Page 197
(9) CB & P   7 August 1693
(10) CB & AD   29 June 1683
(11) CP & P   11 August and 25 September 1692
(12) V   Volume II, page 235
(13) O   Pages 81 - 82
(14) CB & AT   25 July 1705, 25 November 1716 and 8 February 1717
(15) CZ   Volume 7, page 561

Nicolas Pasquin

Chapter 17

Nicolas Paquin
(Pasquin)

*A*fter his arrival in Canada, J. B. Francois Deschamps, founder of the Seigneury of the Riviere-Ouelle, sent a letter to his father Jean in France. "Find me a good joiner for my buildings," said the message. There were joiners aplenty in Normandy, but what qualified joiner would agree to exile himself for three years?

THE CONTRACT

The father of the Seigneur looked for a joiner. At Gemonville he found a serious man who was finishing his apprenticeship at the house of Master Carpenter Jean Balie. His name was Nicolas Paquin. Nicolas, son of Jean and of Renee Fremont, was baptized on 5 April 1648 at the Poterie-Cap-d'Antifer, today in the Department of the Seine-Inferieure. He knew the sea since he had been raised on its shores, facing the Channel; he had heard speak of Canada; could he leave his Normandy, his parents, his sisters Marie, Marthe and Jeanne, in order to go to New France? He discussed the matter with Jean Deschamps and finally accepted what was for those times an advantageous contract. A recruit ordinarily received 75 livres a year, but 13 April 1672, Nicolas signed a three year contract for 150 livres a year. In addition, his Seigneur agreed to pay him forty livres as an advance against his first year salary, provide all the tools of the trade, as well as food, heat and lodging for the duration. Of course, his passage from France to Canada, was paid too.

The deal was made. Nicolas bid farewell to his friends and to his family before leaving for the port of Dieppe, the point of departure toward the great adventure.

AT THE RIVIERE-OUELLE

That year of 1672 was pregnant with events. Madame de la Pelterie, foundress of the Ursuline Order, had died on 18 November 1671. Mother Marie de l'Incarnation, that great mystic, left in her turn, on 30 April 1672. The King recalled the Intendant Jean Talon to France on 2 June and named Frontenac the Governor of the colony on 6 April, 1672.

One summer morning, a 300 ton ship, probably the SAINT JEAN BAPTISTE, sailed up the Saint Lawrence, that flowing boulevard into Canada. Nicolas Paquin left below decks to go foreward to the bow for some fresh air. The setting sun painted magical colors in the west, on the shores, the islands and in the haze. A timorous man becomes a dreamer, seeing only the water and the forest in their beauty. Was this the country? Would the Captain have to stop at Tadoussac to take on fresh water and provisions? An old sea wolf himself, he had said that it might be possible. Where would Nicolas find the domain of his adopted Seigneur?

Nicolas admired the site of Quebec. His Seigneur had to be at the port to greet him. We know that this worthy did not obtain official title to his holding from Frontenac until 29 October; but it seems that M. Deschamps had already begun development the preceding year. Nicolas went to work at the Riviere-Ouelle and scrupulously made use of his contracted time of 36 months in building the edifices for his Seigneur. He never did receive his full salary as we shall see later. He was very sensitive and too politic to provoke a tempest before a court. He was in fact already in love with the country.

ON THE BEAUPRE COAST

After three years at Riviere-Ouelle, Nicolas went to live in the environs of the capital. On 3 July 1676 he acted as witness to the land granted by the town of Beauport. There is no doubt that he worked on the building of the church since we see by his contract that he had become a master joiner.

It was on the Beaupre coast, in the Parish of Chateau-Richer, that he found his future wife, a true Canadienne, Marie-Francoise, conditionally baptized by Urbain Baudry and finally baptized in the home of Sieur Le Tardif by Father Ragueneau, S.J., on 12 February 1655. Marie-Francoise had Jean Plante and Francoise Boucher, inhabitants of Chateau-Richer for a father and mother. The contract of marriage was signed in the house of her step-parents, before Notary Paul Vachon on 20 October 1676. The future husband affixed his signature to the bottom of the contract. November 17th following they made their promises in the presence of Father Jean Gauthier de Brullon; the next day, the nuptial benediction at the Church of Notre-Dame de Chateau-Richer was given by Father Fillon.

The newly married couple were not very rich in material goods. Their courage and their Christian faith served to guarantee them a fruitful future. The Plante parents had properly clothed their 22 year old daughter and they had already given her a milk cow. History does not tell us how the couple lived during those two years at Chateau-Richer, but they did have a child, Nicolas, whose birth record has been lost.

ON THE ILE d'ORLEANS

The land on the Beaupre coast had been all taken up and perhaps conditions for buying a piece were not propitious. In any event, Nicolas opted for the Island of Orleans. On 24 January 1678, he bought land in the Seigneury of Lirec, within the limits of the Parish of Sainte-Famille.

Jean Moreau dit Lagrande, husband of Anne Couture, sold them his farm of 3 arpents frontage, neighbored on one side by Marin Nourrice and on the other by Osannie Nadeau. The obligations attached to this deal were "20 sols of seigneurial rent for each arpent of frontage and one sol "of cens for each arpent of frontage, and, for all the said concession, two live capons" to be sent to the Sieur de Lauzon.

Moreover Nicolas contracted to pay the seller the sum of 600 livres in installments of 200 each, in April 1678, 1681 and 1682. Nicolas Paquin with Michel Montenbeau, Jean Primeau and Notary Claude Auber signed the contract.

The Paquin couple set themselves to the task. Their debts were paid off and the entire family was raised on this farm. They went to the little church of Sainte-Famille built in 1669 on the coast road and canonically dedicated in 1684. The Ile of Orleans is the cradle of the Paquins of America.

FAMILY LIFE

The Paquin parents, during a quarter century, bred 13 children of whom 4 died in the cradle. Additionally, Jean was buried at the age of 2 years, Louis at 1 year and Antoine at 20 years What a painful bereavement! Four daughters built nests: Marie with J.B. Marcotte; M. Madeleine with Jacques Perrault; Genevieve with J.B. Naud and M. Anne with Pierre Groleau. Two of the boys were fruitful: Nicolas and Jean who emigrated to Deschambault. Nicolas, the oldest, was married twice and had numerous descendants. Jean married Marguerite Chapelain in 1731 and was perpetuated by one of his 3 sons, Joseph dit Fichon.

The Paquin couple never left Ile d'Orleans. Nicolas, used up by work, succumbed to the task in 1708 at the age of 60 years. He was buried on 17 December. Son-in-law Marcotte, husband of Marie Paquin, took over the job of supporting his mother-in-law and her children. Three Marcotte girls and a boy grew up with the Paquins. The mother-in-law, Marie Francoise Plante, lived until the age of 71 years. She was buried at Sainte-Famille in April of 1726.

A POSTHUMOUS BOUQUET

The Paquins were a humble, stable, peaceful and charitable family. No lawsuits! No tampering with the inheritance! It seems that their descendants practice the same virtues today.

117

At Sainte-Famille they had an Office for the Poor. It was founded by the Cure Lamy and by Father Auguste Lablanc, S.J. on the 27th of March 1698. By a majority vote, Nicolas Paquin was nominated "Director of Business" and Jacques Bilodeau "Director for Receipts." The first of April Mama Paquin was chosen, with three companions, to beg for charity. Month by month, she collected 18 minots of wheat.

Nicolas Paquin had left Riviere-Ouelle in 1675 before receiving his full salary. There was due him 180 livres, a considerable sum of money for the times. Nicolas was a peaceful man but not easy going; he did not give up his due. Verbally, on 17 October 1700 he made a gift to the Church wardens of his parish of this tidy sum. Only after his death did the wardens bring the debt to the attention of the heirs to the estate of the late Seigneur Deschamps. On 17 June 1710, Notary Etienne Jacob paraphrased a posthumous quittance to Nicolas Paquin and his widow. In return the Society obligated themselves to have 4 Requiem Masses said annually for Nicolas Paquin, his wife, their children and descendants.

These well verified facts form a bouquet of delicate and immortal flowers given to the memory of Ancestor Paquin and his spouse.

RECOGNITION

A monument to Ancestor Nicolas Paquin has been unveiled at Deschambault, P.Q. on 24 August 1975. Brother Pasteur Paquin, S.C., office at 1400 Boulevard de l'Aeroport, Ancienne Lorette P.Q. Canada G2G 1G6, published a well documented book entitled *"Petite Histoire des Familles Paquin en Amerique (1672-1976)."* I have summarized for you the first part of this work, which honors not only the author but also all the Paquins of America.

Pierre Paradis

Chapter 18

Pierre Paradis

All Canadians named Paradis are descendants of Pierre who came to New France in the 17th century. Pierre was a native of Mortagne, the Capital of Perche. His father was called Jacques.

THE FATHER OF PIERRE

Jacques Paradis lived in the Parish of Notre-Dame-de-Mortagne from 1602 to 1612. In 1616 he was in the Parish of Saint-Germain-de-Loyse. On 10 July of the same year, he signed a 3 year lease with the Cobbler Louis Girard, for "a living room with storage loft above the chamber where the lessor is residing; with a shop off to one side for the lessor."

Jacques and his wife, Michelle Pelle, had at least 5 children at Notre-Dame. One was Pierre, Our Canadian Ancestor, who was baptized on 20 July 1604.

PIERRE MARRIES

Pierre Paradis wed the thirteen year old Barbe Guyon about 1633; obviously she was much younger than her husband. Baptized on 19 April 1617, she was the daughter of Jean and of Mathurine Robin, who were married on 2 June 1615 at Saint-Jean-de-Mortagne. It should be said that these parents of Barbe also came to Canada, but in the employ of Robert Giffard.

The Guyon family left France for Canada in company with Robert Giffard in the spring of 1634. Barbe stayed in France with her husband Pierre who worked as a cutler. They did not go with her parents because Barbe had a baby about that time. The child, Charlotte, was born on 4 April 1634 but died shortly thereafter. (1)

A Notary of Tourouve, Jacques Douaire, prepared a receipt for Pierre Paradis, merchant of Mortagne, Parish of Loyse, dated 4 June 1640. It seems that a certain Claude Bailly, resident of Tourouve had ordered, on 11 February 1640, 200 sickles to be delivered on the feast of Saint Jean-Baptiste. Pierre Paradis delivered them on 4 June, that is to say, 20 days sooner, a success! (2)

And here are some more Paradis births in the old country: Marguerite, born 5 February 1636; Jacques, baptized at Notre-Dame on 24 March 1641; Marie, born in 1642; Guillaume, baptized on 26 September 1644; Pierre, baptized at Saint-Croix-de-Mortagne on 2 October 1647; and finally, the last born in France in November 1650 was Jean, the first of two sons by that name. He died at Charlesbourg in Quebec in 1717. There were many mouths to feed, many minds to educate. (3)

PIERRE PARADIS IN CANADA

Pierre Paradis, now an armorer according to Mme. Pierre Mortagne, lived at first at Notre-Dame-de-Mortagne, then at Sainte-Croix in 1643. On 20 March 1651 he and his wife ceded to one P. Richard a little room with a cellar below. This probably was done in view of their imminent departure for New France; because in 1653, they are seen baptizing their ninth child Madeleine, before the font in Quebec.

On 9 March 1654 Pierre bought land from Christophe Crevier; 2 arpents in frontage by 44 deep. (4)

On the first of July 1658 a son Jean was born. Baptized at Notre-Dame-de-Quebec on 22 July, he was destined to become one of the most famous of all the Ancestors. (More about him to follow.)

On 18 March 1667, Pierre obtained another concession near the river, from Sieur Jean Maudry, Surgeon to the King. Called "La Cabane-aux-Taupiers," it was not far from his first property. This small concession of half an arpent in frontage had a house, a garden, a stable and a 30 foot barn. By 1667 the colonist Paradis owned 8 animals and 12 arpents of usable land in the Parish of Notre Dame-des-Anges, not far from Beauport. (5)

According to Notary Romain Becquet, on 7 February 1668, Intendant Jean Talon bought a piece of land that Pierre had acquired in 1654, 76 perches by 18 feet, with the intention to build a road from Beauport to Charlesbourg. Pierre was well indemnified for this right of eminent domain. He received 40 livres in money plus a concession of 40 arpents of land in the new Bourg-Royal. (6)

LAST WILL AND TESTAMENT

Pierre made his will before Notary Becquet on 28 May 1670 when he was gravely ill in the Hotel-Dieu-de-Quebec. (7) He gave 20 livres to the hospital; 20 livres to the Chapel of the Jesuit fathers; 20 livres to the Church of Beauport; his wife Barbe Guyon was to inherit all else without reference to any other custom of inheritance; however Pierre lived for five more years. On 12 July 1672 it seems that he sold his Beauport property to Guillaume Bauche, his son-in-law. (8)

This brave man died at Sainte-Famille on the Island of Orleans, where he was buried on 29 January 1675. Barbe Guyon saw fit to hold an inventory of his personal property at Beauport, before Notary Paul Vachon, on the 3rd of April following. (9) It seems that Barbe Guyon, the widow, lived for many years in the home of her daughter Marie, the wife of Guillaume Bauche, at Sainte-Famille; it is there that we find her in the census of 1681. But later on, she must have lived at Saint-Pierre with one of her sons; she was buried from there on 29 November 1700.

A BEAUTIFUL FAMILY

Pierre Paradis and Barbe Guyon had 12 children, 8 of whom were born in France and 4 at Beauport in the Fief of

Buisson; 3 girls and a boy.

Charlotte, Marguerite and Charles, the eldest children, seem not to have come to Canada since there has been no trace of them even until today. Jacques, Guillaume, Pierre, Jean married to Jeanne Paquet, and, Jean the ship's Captain, married to Catherine Bataille, all had large families and their descendants are scattered throughout Quebec and New England. Madeleine, wife of Nicolas Roussin, died in 1669 in childbirth with her first. Marie-Madeleine merged her life with Robert Charest. Finally there was Louise, who married three times. (10)

Pierre junior is the direct ancestor of Mother Marie Leonie, Alodie-Virginia Paradis, foundress of the Little Sisters of the Holy Family; and of His Excellency Monseigneur Paul Gregoire, Archbishop of Montreal.

The Reverend Mother Marie-Anne-Esther Sureau dit Blondin, Foundress of the Institute of the Sisters of Sainte-Anne (1809-1890), 6th generation, had Louise for her grandmother, the daughter of Pierre Paradis, who was married for the second time at Notre-Dame-du-Quebec on 18 June 1691 to the Ancestor Hilaire Sureau dit Blondin. This Hilaire Sureau was the son of Jacques and of Honoree Pollet, of Saint Hilaire-de-Vouzailles, Diocese of Poitiers. He made his living in Quebec as a carriagemaker.

Pierre Paradis was a sincere and generous Christian. Jeanne Gregoire in her book: *La Source et le Filon* reports this: "One religious ceremony is the distribution of the bread blessed by the priest signifying the pariicipation of the faithful in the divine banquet . . . Pierre Paradis wished to offer something more . . . in the year 1657 he gave a large knife to cut the blessed bread." (11)

According to Tanguay, some descendants of Our Ancestor Pierre Paradis adopted the surnames of Aubin, DesRoches, Dufesne and Devide-poche. (12)

BIBLIOGRAPHY

(1)   AO   Itinerary 7
(2)   BQ   Pages 23, note 60
(3)   DC   Pages 42-43
(4)   CB&H   9 March 1654
(5)   CB&DK   18 March 1667
(6)   CB&K   7 February 1668
(7)   CB&K   28 May 1670
(8)   CB&K   12 July 1672
(9)   CB&DK   3 April 1675
(10)   CZ   Volume 1, page 461
(11)   AM   117 pages. Subtitle: *De l'ancetre Pierre Paradis a la Fondatrice des Petites Souers de la Sainte Famille, Mere Leone*
(12)   CZ   Volume 7, page 575

Captain
Jean Paradis

And now for that seagoing son of Pierre, the second Jean. It is not the practice of this series to go into the second generation, in the belief that each reader will seek out his own lineage if so motivated. However, as a former Captain of four "men-o-war" in my own time at sea, it is a distinct pleasure to honor a fellow mariner of that very special confraternity of those who go down to the sea in command of ships. The following account was written by Roland J. Auger and is reprinted from the *Dictionnaire Biographique du Canada*, V. II, pp. 530 - 531, at the suggestion of the original author, the Reverend Father Gerard Lebel.

Ship's Captain Jean Paradis, was born at Quebec on 1 July 1658, son of Pierre Paradis, cutler, and of Barbe Guyon. He died sometime before 1725 at La Rochelle, where he had settled down.

After some studies with the Jesuits at Quebec, Jean Paradis took maritime courses from Martin Boutet, Royal Hydrographer. Around July of 1678 he bought the two houses of Jean Talon, situated in the Rue Buade at Quebec, bordered in back by the Place d'Armes of the Chateau Saint Louis. He paid the sum of 200 livres; on this occasion Louis Rouer-de-Villeray acted as the agent for Talon who had returned to France.

125

There is no doubt that it was this Jean Paradis who commanded the SAINTE-ANNE, shipwrecked on a sand bar in the river Manicouagan in the autumn of 1704; the Intendant Jacques Raudot ordered the sale of the flotsam from this ship in October 1705. Equally, it was Paradis who was at the helm of the ship NEPTUNE, enroute to La Rochelle, when intercepted by the English Admiral Walker. He was obligated to pilot the Admiral's ship EDGAR into port. One knows the disaster that befell the English flotilla near the Ile-aux-Oeufs. Some historians have blamed the pilot Paradis of negligence, even treason. Treason to whom, since one man's treason is another man's patriotism? He well merits this scornful phrase of Admiral Walker to Colonel Samuel Vetch: "I thank you for having warned me about the French pilot, my confidence in him was indeed misplaced."

Two years later, it would be in 1713, Jean Paradis was Captain of PHENIX departing France for the Antilles, carrying contract labor to those colonies. In 1720. an order from Michel Begon declared good and salable, a hogshead of brandy called "Domaine d'Occident," seized by Etienne Amiot de Lincourt as contraband. Jean Paradis, Captain of the GENEVIEVE, was the smuggler.

Jean died sometime before 1725. He was a resident of La Rochelle where he had married, on 8 June 1693, one Catherine Batailler, daughter of the late Pierre Batailler, himself a ship's captain, and Angelique Roy. They had 8 children of whom a son, also named Jean, became a ship's pilot like his father and maternal grandfather.

Many an ancient mariner has enjoyed the appellation of "Loup-de-Mer". However, this one deserves a special sobriquet, "The Sea Fox".

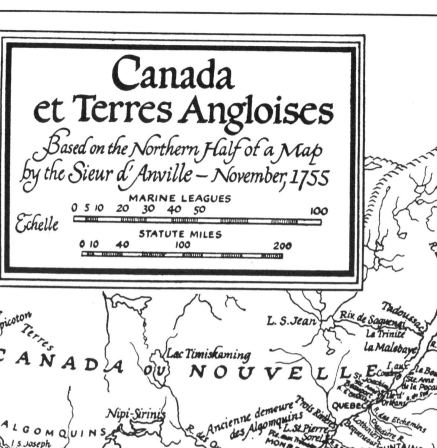

Canada
et Terres Angloises
Based on the Northern Half of a Map
by the Sieur d'Anville – November, 1755

MARINE LEAGUES

0 5 10   20   30   40   50   100

Echelle

STATUTE MILES

0 10   40   100   200

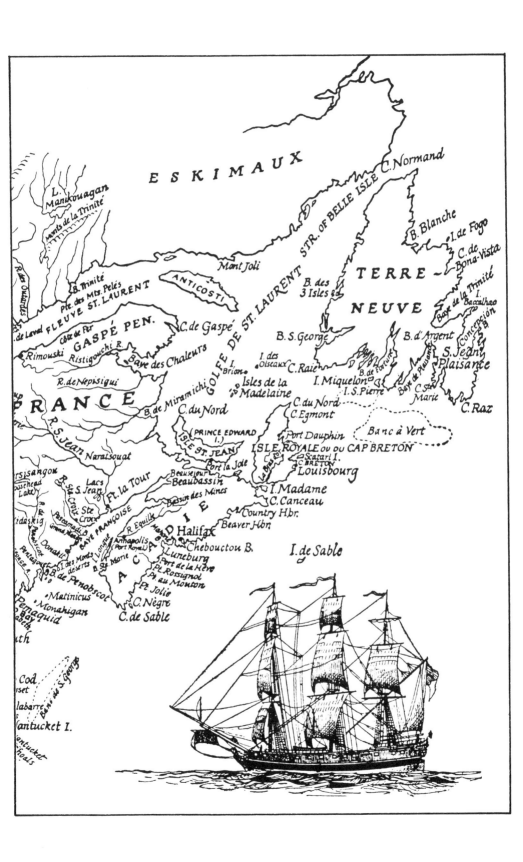

E S K I M A U X

L. Manikouagan

Monts de la Trinité

R. aux Outardes

B. Trinité
Pte. des Mts. Pelés
Côte de Fer
FLEUVE ST. LAURENT

de Laval
Rimouski
Ristigouchi R.
GASPÉ PEN.

R. de Nepisigui

F R A N C E

R. S. Jean
Naraïsouat

rsisangon
bushead Lake
Lacs
R. Ste. S. Jean
Croix Ste.
Croix
Ft. la Tour

idaskig
Grand Man
Passamaq.
Pascat
Donakti
Portagouet
B. de Penobscot
I. des Morts
I. Longue
B. Ste. Marie

Matinicus
Monahigan
Penaquid
ath
uth

Cod
orset
labarre
antucket I.

antucket hoals

Mont Joli

ANTICOSTI

C. de Gaspé

Baye des Chaleurs

B. de Miramichi
C. du Nord

ISLE ST. JEAN
PRINCE EDWARD I.

Port la Joie

Beausejour
Beaubassin
Bassin des Mines
Country Hbr.
Beaver Hbr.
Halifax
Chebouctou B.
Luneburg
Port la Hève
Pt. Rossignol
Pt. au Mouton
Pt. Jolie
C. Nègre
C. de Sable

R. Equill
A C I E

STR. OF BELLE ISLE

C. Normand

B. Blanche
I. de Fogo
C. de Bona-Vista

T E R R E -

N E U V E

Baye de la Trinité
I. Baccalhao
Concepçión

B. des 3 Isles

GOLFE DE ST. LAURENT

B. S. George

B. d'Argent

S. Jean
Plaisance

I. des Oiseaux
I. Brians
C. Raie
B. de Fortun
Baye de Plaisance
C. Ste. Marie

Isles de la Madelaine

I. Miquelon
I. S. Pierre

C. Raz

C. du Nord
C. Egmont

Port Dauphin

Banc à Vert

ISLE ROYALE ou ou CAP BRETON

Scatari I.
C. BRETON
Louisbourg

I. Madame
C. Canceau

I. de Sable

Léonard Pilote

Chapter 19

Leonard Pilote

*Th*anks to some research made in the Archives of La Rochelle by an American nun, Sister Gerardine I. Pilote, author of a work entitled, *"A Pilote Family History (1644- 1900),"* we may now discuss, with considerable more precision, the subject of the life of Our Ancestor Pilote before his departure for New France.

Leonard Pilote married Denise Gaultier at the Church of Sainte-Marguerite de La Rochelle, on 26 May 1644. An Oratorian priest, probably named Preussion, blessed their union. Witnesses: Nicollas Mabillon, Rene Roy, Francois Bazouin and Louys Foucquerai. The Pilote couple had two children that we know of who came to Canada. One was Marguerite Pillot, future wife of Jean Drouart, born the 4th and baptized the 6th of June 1653 by Father Fesquet. They say Leonard's parents were from the parish of Saint-Nicolas de La Rochelle. On 16 September 1657, baby brother Jean Pilote was baptized in the Church of Saint-Sauveur de La Rochelle by the missionary priest Fourre. Godfather and godmother were Jean Barraguay, merchant, and Magdeleine Petit, respectively. (1)

Many ships left the port of La Rochelle each year for Canada. Some of them never returned . . . but on the return of most, members of the crew would tell marvelous stories about the Promised Land. A certain amount of mail also made the shuttle between La Rochelle and the people in that new magical world. Would be emigrants from all over France roamed the streets of this port city awaiting their turn to depart for the unknown.

Leonard, no less than the others, dreamed of New France. He talked it over with his pregnant wife and a decision was made in the spring of 1657: Leonard, with tears in his eyes but hope in his heart, left his family, his town, the port, forever. (2)

On 19 September 1657, we pick up his trail again, before Notary Claude Auber on the Beaupre coast, signing as a witness to a contract of marriage between Our Ancestor Pierre Tremblay and Ozanne Achon. Evidently Leonard did not know that a last child had been born to him. It was the son Jean who was baptized at La Rochelle. (3)

PROSECUTOR

It would be in the autumn of 1658, on 7 October at Quebec, that we find Michel Desorcy, flanked by two witnesses: Julien Martin and Benjamin Auzeau, standing before Notary Guillaume Adouart. (4) This merchant, all decked out in his finery, cut a fine figure of a man, well earning his nickname "Sieur de Boutontrain." He wanted to have a prosecutor assigned to him, really, one of his own! The Royal Notary took up his goose quill pen and in all solemnity wrote a commission for Leonard Pilote, as Prosecutor for Michel Desorcy. At least on paper Leonard now had the power reserved for an emissary of the King! We know from other sources that Michel Desorcy made a business trip back to France. On 27 June 1659, at La Rochelle, he recruited the Ancestor Jean Mathieu for Canada.

Our Prosecutor probably did not carry out his duties during his master's absence; the space of a season. Leonard extracted a promise from Desorcy to make a visit to his wife Denise, living alone in La Rochelle, and bring her all the news. We can even be sure that Leonard sent a letter to his wife by way of Desorcy; it must have been a very long one.

A PROPERTY OWNER

During the winter Leonard Pilote set out to acquire

property for himself. The Squire Simon Denys, "Sieur de la Trinite," husband of Francoise du Terte, ceded him "about 2 arpents of frontage by 30 deep, following the lines . . . of the Seigneury of Notre-Dame des Anges . . . from where the alders begin in that field . . . then following along the great river Saint Laurent. . . ." This act, signed by Notary J.B. Peuvret, on Wednesday afternoon 26 March 1659, also stipulated: the mortgagor (Denys) had bought this land as part of seven arpents in frontage, from the Jesuit Fathers; of which he now had conceded 2 arpents to Pilote, therefore the mortgagee (Pilote) would be responsible for paying each year to the Jesuit Fathers the sum of 8 livres, 15 sols and 2 capons for "cens" and seigneurial rights. In addition, Leonard Pilote was responsible for keeping up the property and building a house upon it. Rene Maheu and Claude Charron applied their signatures as witnesses. Leonard merely signed "PILOT," a name which means "little pillar." (5)

At the end of the contract, a postscript was added and signed by Pilote, to the effect "that he would bring a cord of wood to the farm of the mortgagor during the period of the lease and help the Sieur Denys maintain the roads, fences, etc.," on the property.

Now the Ancestor of all the Pilotes in America had become a landowner. His land was not far from the lower town of Quebec City, and also near that well-organized Seigneury of Beauport. When one owns the land he owns the country.

PLACE ROYALE

Leonard had worked in New France for two years. In the spring of 1659, we believe that he wrote to his wife, living in the Parish of Saint Nicolas, Diocese of La Rochelle, as follows: "Denise, it is here you must come. I have obtained a beautiful grant right next door to Quebec. Join me as soon as you can. My love to Marguerite! How big is Jean now? How goes every little thing with you?"

During the summer of 1660, on 13 August, Leonard signed a two-year lease with Denys de la Ronde, as tenant of a lodging along the Rue Sous-le-Fort, right under the cliff of Cap Diamant, not far from the Champlain stairs, which permitted easy access to the Cote-de-la-Montagne. The rent was 25 livres a year. (6)

Leonard, Denise, Marguerite and Jean were at home on the Place Royale. They did not build that cabin at Notre-Dame-des-Anges as required by the grant.

THE HIRED HAND

In 1662 the house in the Seigneury of Notre-Dame-des-Anges was supposed to be ready as the lease on the lodging in Place Royale ran out. Of course it was not and they had to move.

Just about that time a remunerative job was offered to Leonard. It seems that the widow Etiennette Despres owned a farm of 60 arpents with barn and stable, not far from the Beauport river. This rich lady also had a house in the Place Royale. She was the widow of M. Duplessis-Kergodot, Governor of Trois-Rivieres, killed by the Iroquois on 19 August 1652. Leonard became her official farmer.

A CANADIAN OFFSPRING

On 8 March 1663 a great joy came to the house of Pilote! A son was born. He was baptized the next day by Father Charles de Lauzon-Charney, at Beauport. M. Pierre Denys was godfather, after whom the boy was named, and Marie Anne Duplessis was the godmother.

THE LAST LAND GRANT

On 22 December 1664, Leonard Pilote signed as a witness to the contract of marriage between Charles Garnier (Grenier) and Louise Vezina.

The following year he obtained another concession in the

same seigneury. On 15 October 1665, Doctor Jean Madry conceded 4 contiguous lots to Andre Coudret, David Courbin, Leonard Pilote and again, Andre Coudret. (7)

The descendants of Leonard Pilote will learn with great joy and some surprise that, during this busy period, Leonard and his daughter were among the privileged of Saint-Anne. The first Canadian priest, Father Germain Morin, wrote a treatise in 1687, entitled, "The Miracles that Occured in the Church of Sainte-Anne, as told by the Abbot Thomas Morel." An excerpt read:

> "Leonard Pillehotte, suffering from arthritis for over a year now, having asked for the intercession of Sainte Anne, and having made a pilgrimage there, did receive a perfect cure."

Without a date on it, but beautifully well written, and approved by Monseigneur de Laval, is the following:

> "Marguerite Pillehotte, suffering over all her body for two months now, having likewise asked for the intercession of Sainte Anne, received a cure." (8)

Everything seemed to be going very well. What happened? No one knows, except that a premature bereavement came to strike down this head of family. The death certificate of Leonard has been lost, but we know that he was buried on 3 December 1665 at Quebec, in the cemetery of La Montagne. According to the age given at the time of his marriage, Leonard would have been over forty when he died. He had accomplished much in his short life. Now he would become a concessionaire away up yonder!

A NEW ALLIANCE

Denise Gaultier, after a widowhood of 14 months, married the Norman Robert LeFebvre on 7 February 1667 at Quebec. He was the son of Oliver and of Michelle Renoust of Saint-Nicolas-de-Caen.

Denise did things according to law and custom. On 27 December 1666, she had an inventory taken of the estate of her late husband, made by Notary Paul Vachon in "the house and home of the aforesaid Gautier." Denise became the guardian of her children: Jean, 10 years; Pierre, 5 years; Marguerite, 13 years. The witnesses were David Courbin and Pierre Parent. The surrogate guardian chosen: Jean Drouart. The estate of Leonard amounted to 825 livres and it all reverted back to the children. But on the 24th of December 1667, Christmas gift day, Denise conceded by a notarial act, the sum of 400 livres to her second husband, to be paid to him on her death. If Robert were to die first, this sum would revert back to the children and heirs of the widow Pilote. (9)

This second marriage was without children. The family had no problems with the new head of household installed at Beauport. In 1667 Robert Lefebvre owned 5 animals, 20 arpents of usable land and had a domestic, one Thomas Girard. Their little house was next door to the grand farm of the Jesuits.

After nearly thirty more years of good living, Denise was buried at Quebec on 7 February 1695. Robert survived her by 8 years, until February of 1703.

FROM GENERATION TO GENERATION

The three Pilote children were married at Quebec. Pierre, the youngest, married Marie Jeanne Brassard on 11 January 1694. (10) The couple had only one daughter, Marguerite, who became the wife of Joseph Racine. Pierre Pilote, according to the census of 1681, worked as a domestic for the priests of the Seminary of Quebec. (11)

Marguerite, at 17 years, united her life with that of her guardian Jean Drouart on 20 January 1671. (12) They had only two children: Robert, who was married on 9 May 1707 to Madeleine Page; and Marie-Madeleine, born at the Canardiere, Limoilou, Faubourg de Quebec, and who entered the Ursuline Convent. At the request of Mgr de Saint-Vallier and of his superior, she was assigned to Trois-Rivieres in 1697. After 67 years as a nun, Mother Saint-Michel died at the age of 82 years.

The facts of history tell us that Jean Drouart and Marguerite Pilote his wife, spent the latter part of their lives in the service of the Seminary of Mgr de Laval. The records custodian of the Ursulines reports a most edifying fact on this subject: On the occasion of a fire in the convent of the Ursulines in 1686, Marguerite Pilote, a lay sister of the Seminary of Quebec, freely washed for one year, all the linen of the Congregation soiled by the fire.

It was Jean, born in France, a farmer on the coast of Lauzon, who propagated the name Pilote in America. According to the census of 1681, he owned a gun, a cow and 8 arpents of usable land. He married Marie-Francoise Gaudry on 27 June 1678 and they raised a family of 13 children: 6 girls and 7 boys. (13) Jean, Pierre, Joseph and Charles had heirs. In those days, the traveling missionary recorded official acts wherever and whenever he could. Hence the baptismal certificate of Jean is found in the register of l'Islet; that of M. Francoise in Neuville; and as for the last, J.Ed. Roy writes that she was baptized by the missonary Jean Basset, in the house of Jean Demers (Dumais), on the coast of Lauzon, more precisely at Saint-Nicolas, on 9 July 1688. (14)

One period in the life of Jean Pilote is shrouded in obscurity. After the baptism of his first child on 13 October 1681, and the second, Marie-Francoise, at the baptismal font in the summer of 1688, some seven years are missing. A single contract, signed before a notary on 30 April 1685, gave testimony to the presence of Jean Pilote in the region of Quebec. He had become a *Coureur Des Bois*. Aubert de la Chesnaye was his employer in 1683. Eustache Prevost, second son of Our Ancestor Desrosiers, Martin Foisy, Laurent Benoit dit Livernois, and others, formed the circle of his companions en route to the Illinois. (15) On 8 May 1684, 200 Iroquois attacked 7 canoes loaded with furs. The men in charge showed their letters of permission signed by M. de la Durantaye and M. le Chevalier de Baugy. The Indians didn't care to listen: "This is our country," they kept repeating. After pillaging the canoes, they made prisoners of the entire flotilla, including Jean Pilote. After 9 days of marching, the group approached Fort Saint-Louis des Illinois, where the Coureurs des Bois were released "without provisions, without canoes, no arms other than two old guns with a little powder and lead." Oh, what resourcefulness! On the 28th of May following they were on the plains before Quebec. (16)

One of the notable personages among the descendants of Jean was Monseigneur Francois Pilote, founder of the School of Agriculture of Sainte-Anne-de-la-Pocatiere, in 1859. He was born 4 October 1811 at Saint-Antoine-de-Tilly, from the marriage of Ambroise Pilote and of Marguerite Coulombe. Descendants of Our Ancestor Leonard seemed to be reluctant to adopt other names: only Pilot and Pilotte. (17)

BIBLIOGRAPHY

(1)   T   page 484
(2)   BX   Manuscript records.
(3)   CB & F   19 September 1657
(4)   CB & H   7 October 1658
(5)   CB & BW   26 March 1659
(6)   CB & H   13 August 1660
(7)   CB & DK   15 October 1665
(8)   D   page 14, b. I, 410
(9)   CB & DK   26 December 1666, 27 December 1666 and 24 December 1667
(10)   CB & P   26 December 1693
(11)   I   page 124
(12)   CB & Z   20 July 1670
(13)   CB & CD   31 May 1678
(14)   Lauzon, H.S., Vol. 1, pages 340 - 341
(15)   BG   Volume 31, page 120
(16)   BU   Volume 12, page 284
(17)   CZ   Volume 7, page 578
       DG   pages 101, 136, 137
       BF   Volume 15, page 154
       BM   Volume 14, pages 210, 213, note 83. Volume 15, page 176
       AY.1   Volume 1, page 183

ROYAL NOTARY

Jean–Baptiste Pothier

Chapter 20

Jean-Baptiste Pothier

$\mathcal{T}$he Ancestor of all the Pothiers of Trois-Rivieres and the Cantons to the east was named Jean-Baptiste and signed himself "Pottier."

On his arrival in Canada, this educated young man, originally from Chatres in the Beauce region of France and son of the late Jean and of Marguerite-Sainctes, lived in the Parish of Saintes-Anges-de-Lachine. The Cure Pierre Remy made him the choir leader and schoolmaster of the parish, all for the modest salary of 50 livres per year.

NOTARY

This meager revenue forced our young man to look for more remunerative employment. Where he found it is recorded as follows: (1)

"On 20 December 1686, Jean-Baptiste Pothier received his first contract at Lachine from the Commandant of Montreal who made him his secretary." It was there that he practiced as a Notary for fifteen years. His 353rd Act is dated 26 September 1701, which states, "Donation of a terrain of four and a half perches in width by ten perches in depth by Pierre Remy in the name of the Filles de la Congregation-de-Notre-Dame-de-Montreal, to the people of the parish of Saintes-Anges-de-Lachine." We might add that he was, it seems, the Notary of the Seminary of Ville-Marie, which institution gave him a concession of land on 23 January 1698. (2)

After 23 May 1690, Jean-Baptiste was also the substitute Fiscal-Procurer for the District of Montreal, up until about 1693. That year, then, on 15 March, he became the Royal

Notary in the Government of Montreal. His Commission was registered on 26 March 1695 and his Acts are conserved in the Judicial Archives of Montreal. (3)

In 1701, the region of Trois-Rivieres lost the venerable old Notary Severin Ameau; so the Intendant Bochart Champigny sent for J.B. Pothier. There he went and exercised his profession until his death. He signed 199 Acts, all of which are conserved in the Judicial Archives of Trois-Rivieres, the last dated 21 August 1711. During this three-rivers period, Jean-Baptiste was also Record-Keeper and Jailer in addition to being the Notary. On 17 October 1703, they named him Sergeant-Royal (Sheriff), with jurisdiction over all the territory; taking the following oath of office before the Notary Antoine Adhemar, on 15 March 1704; "And after having taken and received the aforesaid Oath as Royal Sheriff, Pothier is entitled to all the rights and emoluments thereof. . . ." The first of May 1711, the Intendant also added the duties of Judicial Surveyor. (4) In the history of the Ile Dupas, nearby Sorel, it is interesting to read: "The new Seigneurs had a feeling it seems, in favor of establishing some new colonists on the island, therefore on 20 August 1703, they were given concessions before me, Jean-Baptiste Pottier, Royal Notary of the King our Sire in New France, resident of the town of Trois-Rivieres, a property for the use of the cure and on which a church must be built. . . ." (5)

FATHER OF A FAMILY

If public life has its charms and obligations, even more so has family life for a normal man. Jean-Baptiste looked for a companion: on 14 June 1688, he married Marie-Etiennette Beauvais, daughter of Jacques and of Jeanne Solde. Etiennette, baptized on 21 September 1669, was a nineteen-year-old farmer's daughter. (6) The marriage ceremony took place at the Church of Notre-Dame-de-Montreal. Twelve children saw the light of day through this marriage; 7 at Lachine and 5 at Trois-Rivieres, of whom at least 6 died at an early age. An only daughter, Marie-Catherine, married at Montreal; the rest stayed around Trois-Rivieres.

Two boys had children: Joseph-Marie and Jean-Baptiste. (7) The latter, on 14 May 1727, signed on as a Voyageur, to made the trip to Michilimakinac for the sum of 130 livres payable in beaver pelts on his return. (8)

So many bereavements came so often to afflict Etiennette and Jean-Baptiste, especially in their early marriage when they lost their first four children. They loved children, so much so that three months after their wedding they adopted an orphan. The somewhat curious manner of this adoption, in a time when adoption itself was rare, is reported by E.Z. Massicotte: "On 29 October 1688, Pierre Ablin, age 2 years, was contracted out by his father for 15 years to Jean-Baptiste Pothier of Lachine." (9) Annexed to this contract is a piece by the aforesaid Pottier by which he declares "that on 10 January 1692 he gave this child to Marguerite Plumereau, wife of Jean Cardinal and that the new guardian is caring for him as she ought to."

NOT LIKE THE REST

Jean-Baptiste Pothier had an extraordinary legal sense, a meticulous attention to detail in his work, the confidence of the citizens whom he served, as well as the authorities. It was not he who would hunt out of season or cheat in money matters. He had a frank nature, a correct and sturdy character, but perhaps he was too assertive and peremptory to surmount all difficulties. We know that in 1693 there was an exchange of bittersweet words between him and his pastor. The impasse became so serious that on 5 May the Abbot Remy made a complaint about injuries and menace to his person. The matter was settled out of court, to the point that on 31 October 1708, J.B. Pothier even made a sale to his old Cure. (10)

In 1707, Pothier committed an assault upon the person of Madame Noel Carpenter, Jeanne Toussaint de Champlain. He was found guilty and was sentenced to pay damages and interest plus court costs: 100 livres. Moreover, he had to settle the surgeon's bill of 35 livres. (11)

Another time, it was Pothier who was attacked! He received a mean thrashing from the Squire Etienne Pezard de la Tousche. Our Ancestor made him pay dearly: 200 livres in civil reparations, damages and interest. La Tousche made an appeal to the Sovereign Council. The latter, by decree signed 9 February 1705, told him to pay up on the spot. (12)

SUMMER SEASON

Such was Our Ancestor Pothier: an educated man, a worker, quick-tempered, devoted body and soul to his family and country. He does not seem, in spite of all the work that kept him busy, to have accumulated a fortune; quite the contrary! Those little cunning ways that might do well to help a middle-class merchant on his way to wealth, did not have a chance with him, so he was poor! Thus, on 5 October 1695, we see him take a farm, a property of 60 arpents square, at Lachine. This was certainly not for speculation but to balance both ends! (13)

J.B. Pothier died in July 1711 and was buried on the 11th. An eternal summer began for this Choir Master— Glory be to God on High!

As for Etiennette Beauvais, she survived him for more than 40 years. One report had it that she was cured of an illness in 1704 through the intercession of Brother Didace Pelletier. The mortal remains of this pious Brother, who died 5 years later, repose in the crypt of the chapel of the monastery of the Recollets, Rue Notre-Dame, now a Protestant Church. In 1710, Madame Pothier brought twins into the world: Michel and Marie. After the death of her husband, she turned his papers over to the Recollet Father Chauvreau on 8 October 1712. Etienette died in 1753 at age 84 years and was buried on 14 September at Trois-Rivieres. (15)

At Nicolet on 5 May 1834 a descendant of J.B. and Etiennette was born: Louis, son of Claude Pothier and of Josephte Dubois. Louis was ordained a priest at Trois-

Rivieres on 20 September 1863. In 1865 his Bishop named him Cure of Saint Medard of Warwick where, up until his death in November 1897, he carried on a fruitful ministry. He founded a convent for young girls and built a beautiful church which still exists today.

Aram-J. Pothier (1854 - 1928), native to the region of Trois-Rivieres, alumnus of the Seminary of Nicolet, after having become president of a banking institution in Woonsocket, RI, was elected Governor of Rhode Island seven times. This exploit has been equaled only by New York's first governor, George Clinton.

Many descendants of Our Ancestor seemed to have difficulty settling on a family name. Tanguay records no less than sixteen off-shoots: Cordier, DeCourcy, De L'Ardoise, DePoitiers, DePommeray, De St. Germain, Du Buisson, De Poitiers, La Fontaine, LaVerdure, Poiters, Potichon, Potier, Pottier, St. Gemme, and St. Jeme. (16)

BIBLIOGRAPHY

(1)	BF	Volume 32, page 85
		Volume 37, pages 126, 183, 254
(2)	CB & A	23 January 1698
(3)	BO	page 135
(4)	CB & BZ	Inventory of the Records of J.B. Pottier
(5)	BY	page 19
(6)	CB & BK	13 June 1688
(7)	X	Volume III, pages 1822, 1823
(8)	CB & CEI	pages 1 - 228, exact citation unknown
(9)	CB & A	29 October 1688
(10	CB & A	31 October 1708
(11)	BT	Volume V, page 727
(12)	BT	Volume III, IV, passim
(13)	CB & BK	5 October 1695
(14)	CB & A	8 October 1712
(15)	V	Volume II, pages 550, 551
(16)	CZ	Volume 7, page 580

René Rhéaume

Chapter 21

Rene Rheaume

$\mathscr{I}$t is difficult to bring back the Ancestor of the Rheaumes of Canada and contribute all the specifics necessary to do justice to the most colorful and amazing personality of his time in the Quebec region.

HE CAME FROM LA ROCHELLE

Rene Rheaume was born at La Rochelle, capital of Aunis, in 1643. La Rochelle, an important seaport from where a great number of Our Ancestors left for New France, had been the castle-fortress of the Huguenots and Calvinists. Rene Rheaume was a Catholic lad who must have been all of 20 when he left for New France.

MARRIAGE AT SILLERY

It was at Sillery on 29 October 1665, before Father Henri Nouvel, S.J., that Rene Rheaume married Marie Chevreau, daughter of the late Francois and of Toinette Jallee, of the town of Chateaudun, Parish of Saint-Valerin, Diocese of Chatres. The man of Rochelle was the son of Jean Rheaume and of Marie Chevalier, Parish of Sainte-Marguerite of Notre-Dame-de-Cogne. At the time of their marriage, Marie was an orphan from the Beauce region of France. In order to be present at the ceremony the following distinguished persons came to Sillery: the Marquis de Tracy, Monsieur de Corcelles and the Intendant Jean Talon.

Some weeks before, it would be the 9th of October at Quebec, Notary Pierre Duquet had prepared the marriage contract stipulating that the future spouses enter into a community property arrangement which required that any debts existing prior to the marriage did not carry forward into the marriage as a joint responsibility. The orphan Marie Chevreau brought as dowry an estate valued at 200 livres. As an orphan she had come to Canada under the protection of, and dowered by, the King.

Rene lived in a little house in Quebec between the Jesuits and the Ursuline Convent. According to Father Anselme Rheaume, he married at Sillery because he was friendly with the Jesuits and they had friends there.

AN ENTERPRISING CARPENTER

Rene was good at his job of Master Carpenter: his service was in strong demand for over 30 years. The number of contracts testify to his unbounded activity in and around Quebec, especially during the years 1682 and 1683, the most active of his life.

Jean Amyot and Charles Marquis asked Rene to build them each a roof. As for framing out a house, Rene was hired by Jacques Boissel, Nicolas Rousselot, the widow Marguerite Boissel, Hyppolyte Thivierge, Pierre Duquet, Philippe Neveu, Anicet Boyer, the heirs of Bertrand Chenay, Louis de Niort, Sieur de la Norray, and Nicolas Marion. Rene Branche also required the services of Rene for the construction of his barn and Charles Jobin for that of a house in front of the Bishops of Quebec. Jean Le Vasseur himself, also wanted some beams.

The Intendant Demeules, in 1683, called upon the competent Rheaume to "make a palisade of wood in the form of a road . . . in order to retain the land of the road" that runs from the lower to the upper town along the foot of the hill: Price 700 livres.

Toward the end of 1692 Mgr de Saint-Vallier was erecting an enclosure around the garden of the General Hospital of Quebec. He would need "four hundred round cedar poles, ten feet long and not less than six inches in diameter, driven into the earth at least one and a half feet, but extending up at least seven feet, attached one to the other by wooden dowels. . . ." Rene furnished the wood and did the work in six months.

In December 1704, Jean l'Archeveque, a merchant, asked Rene to build, within six months, a little water mill on the River de la Rets, next to his tannery. Price: 400 livres.

Moreover Rene bought and sold many sites in Quebec, doing such business with Charlotte de la Combe, Pierre Biron, Jacques de la Roe, Guillaume Piquefeu, Antoine Caddee, Pierre Maufait, Pierre Jean, Francoise Lavergne, some priests from the Seminary and some of the Jesuits. Rene was everywhere all the time!

MANY LAWSUITS

The old Canadians had the reputation of being quibblers. Rene Rheaume was well-schooled in this fault.

Perhaps Rheaume the carpenter took on too much work and was not able to honor all of his commitments. His energy and his endurance must have had limits. Compulsively, he would leave one construction to start another. In response to the justified complaints and reproach of his creditors, he would resort to violence. It is thus that the better part of his earnings melted like butter in the frying pan of the courts.

Rene Branche, Jean Lemire, Nicolas Marion, Francois Blondeau, Oliver Morel, Charles Jobin and Ignace Lemay were all plaintiffs in costly court cases against Rene Rheaume. It does no good to butt heads with such men as Nicolas Marion dit Lafontaine, a mature and well-informed merchant of Quebec, well-versed in business. Charles Jobin kept on the heels of Rene for several years. He even tried, on 19 October 1693, to get permission to sell a piece of land "belonging to the said Reome, situated in Charles-bourg, adjoining Jacques Bedard on one side."

Rene never did lie before the court. He always told the truth with manifest goodwill. When the time for sentencing would come, he was always distraught by so many obligations. . . . One day, Pierre Du Roy petitioned the Court for redress for some allegedly poor work done by Rene. The Court appointed experts who examined the work; they declared that everything had been done to perfection. Du Roy was sentenced on 8 March 1695 to pay the 507 livres due to Rene.

A SHARP FIGHT

It was during the winter of 1680. Rene was returning from Saint-Joseph d'Orsainville with a sledge-load of wood. Along the road, our man met three other sleighs barring the way. The four men stopped and glared at each other. They were, in addition to Rene, Pierre Morterel, Andre Morin and Martin Moreau. The air was heavily charged. Rene approached Martin Moreau and garrulously said to him: "You told Miss Villeray that I took some wood from her shed!" Moreau denied it. Rheaume impatiently called him a rascal and offered to box his ears. Moreau proudly retorted that he was not afraid of him!

Things went quickly from bad to worse with Rene. He took the offensive with his fists, then grabbed Moreau by the hair, knocking him down so he could get in some good kicks. . . .

They ended up by taking Moreau to the hospital. The next day, Doctor Timothee Roussel found Moreau lying on a bed at the Hotel-Dieu suffering so from his stomach that he could hardly speak.

In the meantime, acting on a complaint from Madame Moreau, Jeanne Lecog, Rene had been put in the royal jail. In his defense Rheaume alleged that Moreau had bit him on the leg . . . The Council sentenced Rene to pay a fine of 20 sols to the King, 20 livres in civil damages to Moreau, to pay 6 livres to the hospital, to pay the doctor bill and court costs of the trial. The defense rests its case!

MULTIPLY YOURSELF WITH CHILDREN

Marie Chevreau and her husband seemed to have lived on the Petite Riviere, along the Saint Charles River, for some 15 years. It is there that the census of 1667 found them with a house and an arpent of cleared land. By 1681 they had 8 children, 10 arpents under cultivation, 1 cow and 1 gun. Then, about 1683, the family moved to the town of Saint-Bernard near Charlesbourg.

Providentially, Marie and Rene had 13 children: 11 boys and 2 girls. Marie-Renee married Michel Renaud of Charlesbourg. Maurice, Robert, Simon, Rene, Jacques and Michel united their destiny with the families Vivier and Giroux, Brunet, Guyon, Catin, Proteau, Gagnon and Amelot.

Rene's last seventeen years were spent in peace and quiet at Charlesbourg. He was hospitalized at the Hotel-Dieu on 16 August 1722. After having received the last Sacraments of the Church, he died on 30 October at the age of about 79 years. Burial the next day took place in the cemetery of Charlesbourg. Saint Peter must have opened the gates of heaven to him without an argument!

We find people of all occupations and of all professions among the descendants of Rheaume. We note that Rene junior was Captain of Militia on the Beaupre Coast. From Windsor, Ontario, came one Joseph Rheaume, the first French-Canadian to receive a portfolio in the government of that province.

Louis Rheaume, O.M.I., native of Levis, Rector of the University of Ottawa in 1916, was consecrated Bishop of Haileybury in 1923. Alfred Rheaume, born at Saint-Roch-de-Quebec in 1863, was Director of the Annals of Sainte-Anne for 10 years. He died of yellow fever at Sainte-Croix des Antilles on 23 May 1902.

The Reverend Father Cyprian Tanguay lists several alternate surnames adopted by the descendants of Our Ancestor: Reaume, Reame, Aleaume, Beaume, Larose, Leaume, Thamur and Themus.

SOME ACKNOWLEDGEMENTS

If I have been able to write this monograph, it is with thanks for the help to my friend, Father Joseph Rheaume, O.F.M. At the turn of the century he was a choir boy at the Church of Saint-Anne-de-Beaupre. Father Rheaume has utilized his leisure time during the better part of a quarter century to compile the work accomplished by Father Anselme Rheaume in documenting the Rheaume family history. Since the documentation is his, not mine, the Bibliography is not annotated.

BIBLIOGRAPHY

CB & K   2 April 1666, 22 July 1666, 6 August 1672, 17 June 1673, 26 February 1674, 17 June 1674, 2 September 1674, 11 December 1674 and 14 February 1677

CB & P   11 May 1697 and 17 May 1714

CB & Z   9 October 1665, 22 December 1676, 24 November 1679, 23 May 1680, 29 November 1681, 22 December 1682, 12 July 1683, 21 October 1683 and 6 December 1683

CB & AH   23 February 1683, 15 March 1683, 20 October 1683, 6 August 1686, 7 March 1688, 6 May 1689, 7 September 1689, 12 May 1690, 10 October 1691, 19 June 1692, 17 November 1692 and 19 May 1704

CB & CD   23 January 1667, 10 April 1676, 14 March 1678, 7 February 1679, 4 July 1679, 7 August 1679, 11 March 1680, 26 April 1680, 18 November 1681, 2 January 1682, 10 August 1682, 25 November 1682, 15 September 1683, 2 December 1683, 15 December 1683, 24 April 1684, 19 May 1684, 30 July 1685, 12 August 1685, 6 August 1686, 24 January 1687, 18 February 1688, 27 October 1688, 10 August 1689, 11 September 1690, 18 March 1691 and 19 March 1696

CB & DK   18 November 1683

Y   page 207

AY   page 34

CL   See Bibliography. The original author, R.P. Gerard Lebel, had the privilege of consulting the original documentation.

CV   Volume I, page 51

CX   Volume 8, page 49. Charles Rheaume. A descendant lives at Green Bay, Wisconsin.

DG   page 115

CE   Volume 49, page 69

BF   Volume 50, page 64. M. Rheaume, Captain of Militia, died in battle on the Plains of Abraham, defending Quebec.

BT   Volume I, pages 562 - 563, 955 - 956
   Volumes II, III, IV, passim

BM   Volume 23, pages 3 - 18

CZ   Volume 7, page 583

Pierre Rondeau

Chapter 22

Pierre Rondeau

 $\mathcal{T}$o the west of La Rochelle, toward Poitou, in the Parish of Marsilly, the clocktower of Fondouce serves as a landmark for navigators. Pierre Rondeau came from this maritime setting in the village of Nantilly. The son of a plowman, Jacques Rondeau, and of Jacquete Paillereau, he was baptized on 6 July 1642. His godparents were Pierre Berbin and Jeanne Brilliot; siblings Jean, Louise, Catherine and Jeanne had preceded him at the baptismal font, with Michel, his younger brother. Pierre never knew his grand-parents, Michel and Sara Comtois, who died before 1623, the year that their estate was settled. (1)

The last we hear of Pierre in France was on 20 May 1663 when he made out his will before Notary Teuleron in La Rochelle. This act probably signaled his intention to embark on the long and perilous trip to New France.

THE DOMESTIC

The name Pierre Rondeau appears for the first time in Canada in the official census of 1666. "The domestics of Monseigneur the Bishop, living on his farm, are listed below: . . . Pierre Rondeau, 28, laborer." Thus we find Our Ancestor at age 28 in the employ of Mgr de Laval on his farm at Saint Joachim in the shadow of Cap Tourmente. This detail allows us to conclude that Pierre arrived in Canada in 1665. Jean Talon ordered the census a short while after his arrival in the country; and it was made at the beginning of the winter of 1666, a season closed to navigation. (2)

At that time, those who came from Quebec to Saint Joachim by boat, debarked at the foot of the Church of the Great Patroness. Pierre Rondeau had his own kneeling bench in the second chapel of Sainte-Anne-de-Beaupre.

THE CONCESSIONAIRE

In the time of the French Regime, he who owned the land owned the country. Our Ancestors had no reluctance to divide New France into Seigneuries, Fiefs and Concessions.

Pierre received his first concession on 2 June 1667, from Mgr de Laval in the "Episcopal Residence of Quebec." For his 3½ arpents of frontage on the river, to the west and not far from the Church of Saint-Jean, Ile d'Orleans, Pierre had to pay 20 sols for seigneurial rent each year and 12 deniers for "cens" for each arpent of frontage, not to forget the 3 live capons due on the feast of Saint Martin, 11 November. His neighbors were Jean Alliare and Jean Roy. (3)

Six years later Pierre had some discussion with the Jesuits about getting sixty arpents of land "in the ile of Reaux near the ile dorleans." The Reverend Father Guillaume Mathieu even saw fit to draw up a contract on 19 September 1673. The agreement remains in the minutes of the Notary Becquet but never was signed. (4)

A second concession, in due form, was offered to Pierre Rondeau on 30 January 1675. The Jesuits of Quebec had owned the Ile-aux-Reaux ever since 20 March 1638; they conceded him half of this island whose total area was 250 square arpents. Charles Fribaut became the owner of the eastern half and Pierre had that half facing the Quebec coast to the west. They both received unlimited rights to hunt and fish; and interestingly enough, the price of this deal, today a paradise for bird hunters, was 12 livres in silver annually plus one live fat capon as seigneurial rent and 1 sol for "cens." It seems that Pierre never did put a cabin on this island. (5)

A BUSINESSMAN

On 8 October 1674, Pierre Rondeau rented a farm from Jean Jouanne. This farm, adjacent to Pierre Filteau's, was not far from his own property. The three-year lease was at an annual rent of sixteen minots of corn and two minots of white peas. Another deal was made on 10 October 1678, between Pierre Rondeau and Charles Fribaut with Guillaume Julien, merchant and butcher living in Quebec. The two friends agreed to deliver 20 minots of wheat for the sum of 90 livres. By mutual agreement between the three contractors, this deal was cancelled without stating any reason. (6)

On 25 March 1680, Pierre Rondeau requested the service of Pierre Coeur dit Jolicoeur, iron worker and locksmith of Quebec. The latter came right into the Rondeau home with his hinges, braces and bindings, his locks and bolts, and even a pothook, all to fix up the hearth of Our Ancestor. In addition to feeding and putting him up, the iron work cost 36 livres. This is the only contract that carried the mark of Pierre Rondeau, a solid and true P.R. (7)

The same year, Simon Rochon (Rocheron), resident of the Seigneury of Lauzon, asked Pierre to plow and plant two bits of land, one on the north and the other on the south side of the Ile d'Orleans. Price for the work would be 80 livres, in addition to which Pierre was entitled to the pasturage and the hay that he could cultivate that year only. The good Guillaume Couture, Captain of Militia of the Lauzon coast, signed as a witness along with Hypollite Thivierge; Romain Becquet presided as Notary. (8)

A NEIGHBOR AMONG NEIGHBORS

Pierre Rondeau had many good friends who would appear as witnesses to his contracts. The name of Charles Fribaut is a good example. However, Pierre got into trouble with Julien Dumont. Pierre and Julien never should have been neighbors. The first bit of squabbling appeared on 21 November 1674. Julien Dumont and Guy Beaudin filed suit against Pierre Rondeau for libels suffered. This suit was dismissed by the Sovereign Council on Christmas Eve of the same year.

Nine years later some difficulty about land boundaries came up. Pierre filed an appeal of a decision rendered by the Sheriff of Orleans Island and the Provost of Quebec. The Appellate Court ordered a new survey by Jean Guyon: this was made on 23 August 1683. Two years later Pierre was ordered to pay the surveyor his fee of 15 livres.

Monday, 26 March 1686, Julien counterattacked. He obtained permission from the Sovereign Council to bring in two surveyors, Guyon and Le Rouge, in order to check the boundary lines between the two neighbors. The 26th of the following April the two men made an appearance in court. Alas for Pierre, he was ordered to pay all of the expenses for having, it seems, altered the boundaries by 2 feet, 2 inches. (9)

A FATHER OF A FAMILY

Pierre Rondeau married the nineteen-year-old Catherine Verrier, daughter of Jean and of the late Agnes Briquet, originally from Saint-Pierre de Courtils, Diocese of Avranches, in Normandy. They were married on 30 September 1669 at Sainte-Famille, Ile d'Orleans. The orphan Catherine was a King's Daughter, according to the historian, Sylvio Dumas. The proof lies in the fact that she brought to her husband an estate valued at 200 livres plus a gift from the King of 50 livres. (10) They say that Catherine Verrier had made an earlier contract of marriage, on 20 September 1669, with the Breton Julien Talua dit Vandamont. The research provided by this contract, annulled 4 days later, permits us to infer the existence of the same details concerning the contract of marriage between Catherine and Pierre Rondeau, which cannot be found. Julien Talua married at Quebec on 7 October of the same year, to the Norman girl Anne Godeby. This couple emigrated to Montreal and was unhappily mixed up in the story of Our Ancestor Roy dit Desjardins. (11)

Pierre and Catherine had 5 children: Francoise, born 1671; married 7 June 1686 at Saint-Jean, I.O., to Jean Daniaux, son of Jean Daniaux and Renee Brunet from Saint-Andre, city of Noirt, Diocese of Poitiers, Poitou, France. Elizabeth was born 10 October 1673 in Quebec. She married 28 April 1692 at Sainte-Famille, to Simon Chamberland, son of Simon Chamberland and Marie Boisleau. Marie, born 1 May 1676, was married 2 March 1699 to Ignace Chamberland, son of Simon Chamberland and Marie Boisleau. Pierre, born 23 May 1679, married 8 November 1700 to Marie Anne Jouin, daughter of Pierre Jouin and Marie Anne Beaujean. He died 20 February 1704. Catherine, born 20 October 1682, married 29 July 1709, to Jean Mimaux, son of Pierre Mimaux and Mathurine Renaut, from Sainte-Croix, Diocese of Poitiers, Poitou, France. (12)

Then a real test of strength hit Ancestor Rondeau in the spring of 1683. In an inventory taken on 14 February 1685, we read that Catherine Verrier "died by accidental drowning while crossing the river through the northern passage on her way to Quebec." This long and precise text of Paul Vachon tells us in touching detail: "in regard to the clothes of the late mother, they will be cut up to provide for the children." Among other things we find in the house; a little feather bed, three old blankets, one made of dog's fur and another of deerskin and a barrel of eels. (13)

Pierre took his courage in both hands and found a second mother for his children. Marie Asselin (Ancelin), the fourteen-year-old daughter of Rene Ancelin and Marie Juin. Marie had been baptized on March 18, 1669 in Chateau-Richer. Rondeau was now forty-one years old and his oldest child, Francoise, was twelve. Today it is very difficult to imagine such a union, but in the seventeenth century in Canada, women were scarce and the legal age of marriage for a girl was twelve. Rondeau's is by no means the only recorded case of a middle-aged man marrying a child bride. However, the contract was made on 22 August 1683 without the bride even being present. On the side of the bride were the following witnesses: Rene Asselin and his wife Marie Juin, Mathurin Chabot, Charles Fribot, Nicholas Audet and Maurice Arrive. For the groom, we find Pierre Filteau, Pierre Blais and Martin Poisson. (14)

The marriage took place on the following 5th of September in the church at Saint-Jean, Ile d'Orleans. They had four children as follows: Etienne, born 19 March 1685 in Saint-Jean, I.O. and married 11 January 1711 to Gabrielle Louise Moreau, daughter of Jean Moreau and Marie Rodrigue (Barbel). Marthe was born 19 January 1687 and died 18 February 1687. Jean, born 7 June 1688, first married on 24 January 1718 at Contrecoeur to Madeleine Guignard, daughter of Pierre Guignard and Francoise Tierce. His second marriage on 21 July 1721 was to Marie Josephte Baillargeon, daughter of Nicolas Baillargeon and Marie Therese Harel. His third marriage on 15 September 1750 at Lanoraie was to Louise Charpentier, daughter of Denis Charpentier and Genevieve Cottu. Joseph was born 1 November 1690 and married 1718 to Jeanne Marie Passerieu dit Bonnefond, daughter of Pierre Passerieu and Marie Therese Marets. (15)

TO THEIR GLORY

Pierre Rondeau had his work cut out for him in keeping two wives happy, raising two families and accumulating whatever he could lay by. An early death seemed predictable and with no surprise he passed away toward the end of the year 1691, at 49 years of age. Marie ordered an inventory of his belongings on 24 January 1692. We have never located the death certificate nor the burial record of this Ancestor especially noted for his spirit and initiative. He left 8 children to mourn him, whose descendants today are most numerous, especially in Quebec. (16)

Marie, widowed at the age of 22, still had seven children at home. Her oldest stepdaughter was already married and Elizabeth, the second oldest was to be married on April 28. Remaining at home would be Marie, 16; Pierre, 13; Catherine, 10; Etienne, 8; Jean, 5, and Joseph, 2. It is not difficult to imagine the hardships that she must have undergone in trying to manage the farm and rear the children.

Later, Marie met a soldier by the name of Pierre Fournier de Belleval. They were married on July 30, 1693 in Quebec. Fournier, 30, was the son of Jacques Fournier and Ursule Gaucher from the Parish of Saint-Victor, Diocese of Orleans, in France. Fournier had been in the Canadian army for four years and seems to have served in the French army prior to this. In 1700 he was commissioned an infantry officer, rank of Ensign. In the colonial service in 1701, there were 23 Ensigns for 28 Companies. In 1708 he was an Ensign of the Lorraine Company. That year Pierre and Marie appointed Julien Boissy de la Grillarde, master pastry cook of Quebec, as their agent to collect 10 livres in annual rent from their son-in-law, Simon Chamberland, and 200 livres from Michel Fortier in return for the sale of some land. The burial record of Marie, mother of 13 children, has not been located. (17)

A few of the descendants of Our Ancestor took other surnames, (18) i.e., St. Laurent and St. Sauvin, but one Rondeau deserves an honorable mention. He is Father Pierre Rondeau, son of Pierre and of Marie Levesque of Berthier. Ordained in 1857 after a year as a Professor at the College of Terrebone, he brought his missionary zeal to Vancouver Island. He also served as Chaplain to the Sisters of Saint-Anne and worked with the Indians of Chamigan for more than 40 years. In 1870 this missionary Rondeau tended cows and sold butter in order to earn the money needed to build a little chapel dedicated to Saint-Anne. This chapel came to be called the "Church of Butter" as a result. Father Rondeau was buried among his flock on 11 April 1900. Visitors to the little chapel will still find a portrait of him put there by his Indian congregation.

BIBLIOGRAPHY

(1)	CE	Volume 53, pages 259 - 260
(2)	BM	18: 1 & 2 (January - April 1967): 7 - 116
(3)	CB & DK	2 June 1667
(4)	CB & K	19 September 1673
(5)	BF	Volume 2, page 88
(6)	CB & CD	10 October 1678
(7)	CB & Z	26 February and 16 June 1680
(8)	CB & K	12 June 1680
(9)	BT	Volume I, pages 890 - 891
		Volume II, pages 886, 890, 1017 - 1018
		Volume III, pages 17 - 18, 22 - 23, 34 - 36
(10)	Y	page 344
(11)	CX	Volume 4, page 54, col. b; page 73, col. b.
(12)	CM	pages 107 - 108
(13)	CB & DK	14 February 1685
(14)	AC	pages 47 - 48
(15)	CM	page 109
(16)	CB & AS	27 January 1692
(17)	CB & Z	Volume 5, page 87, col. a.
(18)	CZ	Volume 7, page 586
(19)	BF	Volume 1, pages 144, 157, 172, 179

Vue de Québec - 1864

Simon Savard

Chapter 23

Simon Savard

$\mathcal{T}$he Ancestor of the Savards of America, Simon, lived in France at Montreuil-sur-Vincennes, Parish of Saint-Pierre, today Montreuil-sous-Bois, near Paris. It was on this spot on 15 June 1644 he married Marie Hourdouille. It was at Montreuil-sous-Bois that the couple "Savart" had 6 children: 3 girls and 3 boys. Simon junior was baptized on 10 August 1654; and Jean on 7 October 1657. Without a doubt it was to better house his family, that Simon Savard bought the home of his brother-in-law, Eustache Hourdouille, husband of Jeanne Joignaux. The house was located in the Rue Cuve du Four in Montreuil, today the street is named Alexis Le Pere. This contract, dated 23 July 1650, is conserved in the French National Archives, wherein the profession of Simon is indicated to be that of carriage-maker; and his brother-in-law is a drayman. (1)

In the spring of 1663, Simon Savard and Marie Hourdouille, after 19 years of family life in Paris, decided to better their condition and emigrate to New France. It took a lot of courage to emigrate; at that time the risks of the ocean crossing were much greater than our astronauts take today on their trips to the moon.

PERILOUS CROSSING

All indications are that the family Savard went to La Rochelle about 20 April 1663 in order to embark on one of the ships leaving for Quebec. Captain Guillon was Master of the FLUTE ROYAL, out of Brouage, commanding a ship of 300 tons; Captain Gargot, commanding the AIGLE D'OR of the same tonnage. In addition to baggage and provisions, 150 people were packed like sardines between decks of each vessel. Only the captains had a private cabin.

Evidently salt pork replaced filet mignon in these floating palaces and after several days at sea potable water hardly merited the name. Those who could survive managed to arrive. Sickness struck down the majority of the emigrants with death reaping many. "We had to leave 75 at Plaisance on the Isle of Terreneuve and 60 died at sea, therefore we debarked 165 at Quebec, among whom were 6 families composed of 21 people." There is no mention of any particular details concerning the Savard family but all indications are that Simon was severely indisposed during this voyage and his health was dangerously undermined.

A PRECARIOUS BEGINNING

The Savard family touched Canadian soil during the summer of 1663. Were there any friends to greet them? In general they say that the new arrivals were received with universal rejoicing. Moreover charitable help provided by government organizations facilitated the rapid placement of the new citizens. Marcel Trudel in *Le Terrier du Saint Laurent* affirms that by the end of the same year Simon Savard had been granted a concession in the rear row of the Fief of Charney-Lirec on the Isle of Orleans, in the Parish of Saint Pierre. This concession of 3 arpents of frontage was bordered by that of Jean Bourdon. We find it difficult to believe that Simon had the time or the strength to put up a cabin before the winter set in.

Since luck was not with him, on the first of March 1664, he had to ask the Sovereign Council to help him and his five children survive. According to the census of 1666, Denise the eldest at 23 had married Our Ancestor Abraham Fiset, on 5 February 1664 at Chateau-Richer. He was a carpenter from Dieppe presently residing at the Ange Gardien. Simon had the satisfaction of being granted his request, as attested to in a letter dated 18 June and addressed to the King by the Sovereign Council: "As for staple food and other commodities such as clothing, shoes, blankets ... we have distributed them to families for their subsistance... upon a request presented by Simon Savart pertaining to this, stating that he was in need of assistance for himself, wife and 5 children, staples were taken from the stores that the King sent last year for the relief of new inhabitants . . ." It was Sieur Jean Bourdon who carried out the order to help the Savards. (2)

In the spring Simon Savard's belongings were moved to Beauport where he had already gone and it was there that he died. Notary Paul Vachon took the inventory on 15 August 1664. We have not been able to consult this document, probably lost, but we know from the contract of marriage of his widow, made by the same notary, that Simon was a Carriagemaker and Citizen of Beauport.

MOTHER AND DAUGHTER MARRIED THE SAME DAY

Marie Hourdouille had to provide for the needs of 5 children: Francoise, Simon, Jean, Francois, and the little Marie, age 4 years. A suitor knocked at the door: Jean Rheaume, the 22 year old son of Guillaume and of Catherine Le Moyne, originally from the Parish of Saint-Nicolas-des-Champs, some kilometers distant from Montreuil-sous-Bois.

In January of 1665 at La Clouterie, (the name of the rear-fief of old Zacharie Cloutier) the parents and friends of Savard-Rheaume got together. Jean Rheaume promised to take Marie Hourdouille as his lawful wife and do the best he could for her and her children. He accepted them as his own until each should be fifteen years old. Moreover he assured Marie's future with a dowry of 800 livres in event of death. Jean Rheaume signed first: his beautiful handwriting indicated him to be a man of intelligence, delicacy and education. (3)

Two days later before the same notary, the 14 year old Francoise Savard signed her contract of marriage with Robert Jeannes, navigator, a Norman from Rouen, now an inhabitant of the Isle of Orleans and neighbor to his father-in-law Jean Rheaume. The two marriages, that of the mother and the daughter, were recorded in the register of Quebec on the same date, 26 January 1665.

GRANDMOTHER ALONE

On 22 January 1665 Jean Rheaume bought some land in the Seigneury of Lirec on the Island of Orleans, between the lots of Mathurin Chabot and Robert Jeannes, four days after his marriage to the widow Savard. Then the couple set up housekeeping at first on the land left by Simon Savard. (4)

According to a popular saying, the first spouse is a husband, the second is a friend. Was this true for Marie Hourdouille? We know that they had a daughter Marie-Madeleine Rheaume, baptized 21 May 1666 at Charlesbourg who died in the cradle. After the census of 1666, Jean Rheaume lived on the Beaupre coast with the Savard children (5) with the exception of the 8 year old Francois who lived with his sister Francoise on the Isle of Orleans. Then we hear nothing more about Jean Rheaume. Father Archange Godbout believes that he returned to France. Was he shipwrecked? At the census of 1667, the Savard children were living in the home of Nicolas Roussin.

At the time of the marriage contract between Jean Savard and Marguerite Tremblay, made before Notary Etienne Jacob on 24 March 1687, there is no mention of his stepfather, even though Marie Hourdouille was present. The census of 1681 tells us that the family Savard was installed at La Petite Auvergne, Charlesbourg, where they owned 2 guns, 4 head of cattle and 10 arpents of usable land. Nicolas Dupont de Neuville had given this concession to Marguerite. (6) So it would seem that the family was managing quite well. The boys Simon and Jean were living in the Charlesbourg area. Apparently Jean had served as a domestic in the house of Pierre Gagnon at Chateau Richer. Marie Hourdouille lived at Charlesbourg up until her death. She was buried on 25 November 1703.

FALLOW LAND

If the name Savard means fallow land, that's not to say that it applied to Our Ancestor. Simon junior married Francoise Tellier; they had 14 children, of whom 10 married near to Charlesbourg. As for Jean, more unstable, less chance for love in his life, two contracts of marriage were annulled. Eat the oats twice, they say (8) — he married 3 times and was father of 15 children. His eldest Joseph-Simon, first colonist on the Ile-aux-Cedres, married Marie-Josephte, daughter of the ancestor Guillaume Morel, on 27 July 1711, at Sainte-Anne-de-Beaupre. This couple moved toward the Baie-Saint-Paul area early. In the first register of the Ile-aux-Coudres, one finds an entry written on the occasion of the marriage of Brigitte Savard with Barthelemi Therrien in 1743, affirming that Brigitte is the first person born in 1720 near the Riviere-des-Pruches, before the date of the first concession, 6 July 1728. The better part of the Savards of Charlevoix and of Saguenay descended from Joseph-Simon, son of Jean, grandson of Simon the Ancestor. (8)

The same Joseph was named Lieutenant of Militia and Commandant at the Isle-aux-Coudres, by an order signed on 30 January 1731. He was also a qualified Saint Lawrence River Pilot, as attested to by a certificate delivered to him by M. Testu de la Richardiere, Port Captain of Quebec. The order, dated 27 August 1737, qualified him to pilot ships from Cap-aux-Oies up to Quebec.

FIRST FLOWER

The first Canadian priest to bear the name of Savard was called Louis, son of Bernard and of Zoe Boily. He was born on 21 April 1851 at Sainte Etienne-de-la-Malbaie. After having been ordained by Monseigneur D. Racine in April 1878, he became Vicar at Baie-Saint-Paul for 2 years, then at the Cathedral of Chicoutimi for 3 years. Afterwards he became the Cure of Saint-Fulgence.

On 13 November 1884, another Louis Savard repaired to the novitiate of Saint-Trond in Belgium, took his religious vows and also took the oath to be a Redemptorist until his death. From 1885 to 1888 he exercised his ministry at Saint-Anne-de-Beaupre. Following that, he worked at Sainte-Anne of Montreal. During a great mission preached in the city in December 1899, he was stricken by paralysis. He was able to improve a little but then died on 11 September following.

Father Savard was an amiable confrere, a delicate and faithful religious, a sacerdotal flower.

BIBLIOGRAPHY

(1)	CK	1976, page 440
(2)	BT	Volume I, page 126
(3)	CB & DK	12 January 1665
(4)	CB & AH	9 November 1686
(5)	CX	Volume IV, page 55 - 57
(6)	CB & CD	7 June 1671
(7)	CB & AH	28 February 1687
(8)	CZ	Volume I, pages 543 - 544
	CQ	Pages 34 - 36 and 365
	BF	Volume 48, page 320
	BM	Volume I, page 255 - 258

Etienne Trudeau

Chapter 24

Etienne Trudeau

$\mathscr{E}$tienne Trudeau, the Ancestor of all the Trudeau, was said to be the son of Francois, Master Mason, and of Catherine Matinier, of Notre-Dame-de-Cogne, in the city of La Rochelle. He had been baptized in another parish of the same city: Sainte-Marguerite, on 15 September 1641; the godparents were Etienne Vilain and Catherine Boulliot. This robust fellow, a Master Carpenter at 18 and already noted for his fine work, decided to try an adventure in Canada. On 8 June 1659, before Notary Demontreau and Jerome Le Royer, the Representative of M. de Queylus, he signed a contract "to do five years of military service in New France." (1) Etienne left La Rochelle on 2 July 1659 aboard the SAINT-ANDRE, a ship of 300 tons. Also aboard during the same crossing were Marguerite Bourgeoys, Jeanne Mance and two Sulpicians. (2)

WORK AND HONOR

After his arrival at Montreal, Etienne was placed in service to the Sulpicians, for which he was hired. They had a concession named Sainte-Marie, with a house for workers not far away, situated about a mile and a half from Ville-Marie, the original name of Montreal. On 6 May 1662, circumstances gave Etienne an opportunity to distinguish himself by his bravery. Here is a resume of the event as reported by the historian Faillon.

"Fifty Iroquois hid themselves in a nearby woods in order to surprise some of the men from Sainte-Marie. That evening, nearly all of the workers had returned to the house, except three: Trudeau, Roulier and Langevin. These last were approaching the safety of the house, a miserable hole honored by the name, where a sentry should have been on guard, when, without a sound, a band of Indians stood up and raised their guns. At this same moment one of the three cried "To arms, the enemy is on us." The Iroquois commenced firing while our men quickly made for the redoubt. Le Sieur Trudeau, very big and strong and with proven courage, encountered the fleeing sentry and with some kicks and cuffs got him back into the house. Then began what was for one side a furious attack, and for the other a spirited defense: the Iroquois fired repeatedly and stormed the position while the defenders on their side responded with intrepid confidence and always with pity for the Iroquois who, after having fired over 300 shots, had no more advantage than having cut the weapon of Roulier in half."

The firing was heard at Sainte-Marie. M. de Belstre, with all available men, came to the rescue of the redoubt. Seeing this, the Iroquois retreated, taking their wounded with them. This scene took place on ground located today between the Rue Sainte-Hubert and Amherst Street.In order to commemorate this brave act, a plaque of marble has been put up on the northwest corner of the Rues Lagauchetiere and Saint-Andre. (3)

In 1663, Maisonneuve improved the defense of Ville-Marie. On the first of February a local defense force was organized, composed of 20 squads of 7 men each, whose duty it was to defend the valiant population of Montreal. Etienne Trudeau was made a part of the sixth squad of the Brigade de Sainte-Famille, under the command of Corporal Gilbert Barbier.

A BEAUTIFUL ALLIANCE

Etienne Trudeau married Adrienne Barbier on 10 January 1667. Charles Le Moyne was present, as was the father of Adrienne, Gilbert Barbier, a carpenter. He had been one of the group of 12 colonists who arrived at Montreal in August of 1642. He was also procureur-fiscal and the first warden of the Church of Notre Dame, appointed 21 November

1657. (4) The mother of Adrienne, Catherine La Vau, was a pious woman: later on she wrote a three line declaration claiming to have been cured of a stomach ailment from which she had suffered for 5 years, by the Brother Didace. (5) Five ecclesiatics then added their signatures in attest to this document, which still exists. Marie, a sister of Adrienne, entered the Congregation of Notre-Dame in 1678 and died there on 19 May 1739. Two Barbier sons gave their lives for their country. Nicolas was killed at La Prairie in 1691 in combat against the English. Charles-Henri, perished that same year at Repentigny under the command of Lemoyne de Bienville, in a fight with the Iroquois. A third brother, Gabriel Barbier, accompanied La Salle in 1682 when he discovered the Mississippi. (6)

The Trudeau couple had fourteen children: a daughter Marie married to Jean Arnaud, and 13 boys. Nearly all of them established a family. Francois, baptized in 1673 was in Louisiana in 1706. A document exists in Chicago, signed on 25 July 1710, stating "Acknowledgement of this by Claude Parent and Jacques Langlois in favor of Francois Trudeau, payable at Wabash." (7) In addition to Francois, three other sons of Etienne plied the trade of Voyageur, so as to enjoy a little adventure in the West before settling down to marriage. The so called "service contracts" are numerous in the files of Notary Antoine Adhemer. (8) On 31 July 1688, when he would have been 19, Pierre hired out to Nicolas Perrot, to make the trip to the Maskoutin Indians of the Nadoussin region. Four years later, on 8 April 1692, we see another contract to make a trip to the Outaouais. Then on 10 November 1698, having accumulated a stake in the fur trade, Pierre married Marie-Charlotte Menard at Montreal.

In his turn, Jean-Baptiste signed a contract on 25 May 1701, to canoe out to the Outaouais. Then on 10 September 1701 he paddled down to Detroit by way of Lake Erie. He must have done well enough, for on the first of September 1715, he married Madeleine Parent at Montreal.

Finally Toussaint hired out for a trip to Lake Erie on 10 July 1703. He too must have acquired a stake because he married Barbe Gouyou at Longueuil on 23 November 1715.

Eight of the boys married at Montreal and three at Pointe-aux-Trembles. All of the brothers were equally prolific, as a result their descendants are most numerous today. One of the most notable of these is the Prime Minister of Canada, the Honorable Pierre-Elliot Trudeau, ninth generation son of Charles-Emile, a lawyer, and of Grace Elliot. (9)

CARPENTER AND MASON

Without a doubt Etienne Trudeau would like to have lived solely by his trade as a Carpenter, but this was not to be. In those times even notaries had to resort to the plow and sickle to make ends meet. On the expiration of his contract as a mercenary soldier, Etienne was conceded a piece of land at Montreal on 10 January 1665. (10) On 5 December 1667, Jean Auger-Baron employed Gilbert Barbier, assisted by Nicolas Gode and Etienne Trudeau, to construct "A building of log on log on the second hill toward the woods." This building was intended as a redoubt for defense and was built accordingly. Dimensions were 24 feet long by 18.5 feet wide by 9 feet high, with a door, two windows, a roof, some gables, with loopholes in the front back and sides for sighting on foot. It was named the redoubt of the Sainte-Enfant-Jesus. (11)

On 15 January 1673, Etienne obtained an apprentice license from Jacques Cardinal (12), allowing him to practice the stonemason's trade. In fact, on 19 November 1675 he made a business deal with Antoine Regnaud dit Desmoulins for some masonry work.

On 12 March 1675 he received a concession at Longueuil of 3 arpents of river frontage by 20 deep. His new property was bordered on one side by that of Jean Robin and on the other by the butcher Francois Blot. Would he immediately exploit his new lot? Perhaps in his spare time and for wood, but in 1684, he left for Boucherville where his children were baptized in the church on the south shore.

Etienne did not believe in notaries. He resorted to their service only three times to conclude some sales or other business. Many contracts were merely attested to personally. For example, on 23 August 1688, he obtained a piece of land from the clergy of the Hotel-Dieu of Montreal without a notary.

Etienne Trudeau seemed to have lived an active life up to the age of 70 years. On 6 December 1709 he went before the Notary Antoine Adhemar to settle an obligation from Etienne Trudeau to Toussaint Trudeau, his son. That same day he and his wife retired "to a high room in the house of Marie Trudeau," their daughter, with father Etienne "in a bed, sick in body but sound in spirit." Later, the couple spent 9 years with their son Charles and his wife Madeleine Loisel on the farm of Etienne at Longueuil, which henceforth would be managed by his son. The donation called for the son to take care of the old folks by giving them butter, milk, and eggs, in addition to wheat, peas, etc. For this the son was heir not only to the land but also to 4 oxen, 6 cows, 2 horses, 4 pigs, 6 ewes and 24 chickens. (13)

Etienne Trudeau died at Montreal where, on 22 July 1712, he was buried. An active, brave, talented man was no more. On 19 December 1717, Adrienne Barbier proceded to partition the considerable wealth that remained to her among her children. Then she retired to the home of her son, Jean-Baptiste, where she occupied a room until she died. The death certificate of grandmother Adrienne has never been found. (14)

Descendants of Our Ancestor Pierre Trudeau have taken the surnames of Barbier, Trudeau, Trutaut and Truto. (15)

"O Canada! Land of our ancestors, your brow is garlanded with glorious flowers."
A.B. Routhier

BIBLIOGRAPHY

(1) AB   pages 93 - 95
(2) AA   Volume II, pages 353 - 354
(3) AZ   page 81
(4) BO   *Curious Facts on the History of Montreal*
(5) CB & BD   14 February 1708 and 6 December 1709
(6) AU   pages 57 - 61
(7) BM   Volume 27, pages 195 - 214
                Volume 29, pages 163 - 169
(8) CB & A   to August 1668, 4 November 1692, 26 April 1693, 6 October
                1693, 24 February 1694, 25 January 1696, 7 October 1696, 3
                March 1697, 19 August 1697, 4 September 1697, 7 October
                1697, 8 June 1698, 17 November 1698, 17 August 1699
(9) X   Volume III, pages 1910 - 1913
(10) BP   page 9
(11) BF   Volume 49, pages 277 - 278
(12) CB & J   8 April 1663, 1 October 1663, 20 July 1670, 23 January 1672, 15
                January 1673, 12 November 1673, 19 November 1673, 2
                January 1675, 19 November 1675, 2 July 1676, 23 August 1688,
                3 January 1700, 6 January 1700, 10 November 1700, 18
                November 1701, 26 or 28 November 1702, 23 May 1707, 3
                November 1709, 6 December 1709
(13) BM   pages 209 - 210
(14) CB & BD   19 December 1717
(15) CB & CZ   Volume 7, page 598
      CB & M   11 September 1686
      CB & BR   21 July 1664 and 28 July 1666
      AI   pages 232 - 233
      AJ   *LaRecrue*, 1659, pages 130 - 139
      AY   page 285
      CX   Volume 4, page 76, col. c.
      DG   page 454
      AR   Volume I, page 40
      BF   Volume 33, page 434
      BG   Volume 34, page 165
      CJ   Volume II, page 389

"A VOYAGEUR TRUDEAU"

SEIGNEURIAL NOTARY

Paul Vachon

Chapter 25

Paul Vachon

$\mathscr{P}$aul Vachon, born about 1630, son of Vincent Vachon and of Sapience Vateau, was a native of La Copechagniere, a town in the Department of the Vendee, Arrondissement of La Roche-sur-Yon, Canton of Saint-Fulgent, Diocese of Lucon, in the ancient French Province of Poitou. Paul made the crossing to Canada in 1650 at the age of about 20 years. On 22 October 1653 he married Marguerite Langlois at Quebec. This young country girl, a native of Beauport, was baptized at the Chapel of Quebec, the only one in the region at that time, by the Reverend Father Nicolas Adam, S.J., on 3 September 1639. Marguerite Aubert, the wife of Martin Grouvel, was her godmother. This 14-year-old fiancee, from a dignified family of New France, that of Noel Langlois and of Francoise Garnier, had lived in the region of Quebec since the spring of 1634. (1)

Paul Vachon certainly had an extraordinary education, as we shall come to see later. However, his handwriting, even after three centuries, always gives his readers cause for suffering!

A MAN OF MANY TALENTS

Paul Vachon had many different trades it would seem, one of which was masonry. In 1654, in company with Mathurin Roy, he built the chapel and some sick wards of the Hotel-Dieu of Quebec, whose first stone was laid by the Governor-General Jean-de-Lauzon. (2)

On 14 June 1665, (3) the Seigneur Giffard gave Vachon a concession in the town of Fargy in the Seigneury of Beauport. The area of this first concession was doubled 9 years later on 29 December 1664. Paul Vachon always gave special attention to his farm. In 1666, Michel Aubin, 22 years old, was his indentured servant. At the census of the following year, Paul owned 7 head of cattle and 20 arpents of cleared land. Fourteen years later, another census noted 35 arpents in use, 13 cattle, 1 pistol, 2 guns and a 61 year old domestic named Pierre in his service. Moreover, Vachon had obtained from Charles de Lauzon-Charney, the 12th of August 1660, a bit of land with 4 arpents of frontage, in the parish of Saint-Pierre, I.O. (4) Thomas Le Seuer was his trusted farmer on the spot; Maurice Crepeau and Charles Courtois his good neighbors. Paul sold this farm on 14 September 1678 to Denis Roberge who gave it up on 21 November 1679. (5)

If Paul Vachon needed the help of hired hands on his farms, it was because his other work required it. The principal profession of Vachon was that of Seigneurial Notary. (6) One of his descendants, Andre Vachon, historian, found an act of 23 October 1655 in the Archives of the Sovereign Council, making reference to the title of Notary of Notre-Dame-des-Anges. The second piece known to have been by Vachon, carried a date of 24 March 1658, entitled as follows: "Concession of Jesuits to Francois Truffe dit Rotot." About that time Paul was "Procurer-Fiscal" of the Seigneuries of Lirec and the Ile of Orleans, Secretary to Charles de Lauzon and Recordkeeper for the Seigneuries of Beauport and Notre-Dame-des-Anges, nearby Quebec. Then on 10 November 1667, Monseigneur de Laval named him "Procurer-Fiscal" and Notary in the Seigneuries of Beauport and Isle of Orleans; functions that he conscientiously carried out until he retired in 1693. His last contract, signed on 2 November was simply titled: "Transaction of Michel Giroux and of Jean-Paschal Prevost." (7)

A BEAUTIFUL FAMILY

Paul and Marguerite had 12 children: 5 boys and 7 girls. The first 8 had their baptisms registered at Notre-Dame of Quebec, 3 of whom had been baptized at the little chapel in Beauport: Louise, born 25 May 1662 and baptized the 28th of the same month by M. Charles de Lauzon, Sieur de

Charney; Charlotte, born 12 September 1666 and baptized the 18th by the Abbot Louis Angro; Pierre, baptized in the chapel of Beauport by Guillaume Mathieu, S.J., on 31 May 1671. The baptismal records of the last 4 children are at Beauport.

Marguerite, Louise, Madeleine and Francois married respectively to J.-R. Duprac, Leonard Paillard, Raphael Giroux, Jean de Espinay. As for Charlotte, we know only that she was still living in 1681. Vincent, Noel and Pierre married into the families Cadieux, Giroux and Soulard. All these marriages were celebrated at Beauport. (8)

The eldest of the family, Paul junior, was one of the first priests born on Canadian soil. Native of Beauport, and conditionally baptized at the house by Jean Creste, then officially baptized at Quebec on 9 November 1656 by Joseph Poncet, S.J., Paul pursued his studies at the Seminary of Quebec. He was raised to the dignity of a priest by Mgr de Laval on 21 December 1680. Father Vachon served the South Coast as far as Cap-Saint-Ignace in 1683, and the North Coast from the Grondines to Batascan. He was named Canon of the Quebec Chapter in 1684. In 1692 he served as Cure of Cap-de-la-Madeleine. The church of this three rivers parish, today a center for pilgrimages, was constructed under his direction in 1717. Canon Vachon died on 7 March 1729 and was buried in the sanctuary of the Church of the Cape. They exhumed his body in 1895, only to find him perfectly conserved. (9)

Most of the descendants of Our Ancestor Paul Vachon are evidently known under the name of de Vachon. We find them most numerous today in the Beauce. The family branches stemming from the son Noel often have adopted the surname Pomerleau; those of the line from son Vincent sign themselves dit Laminee. A few even use the name Desfourechettes. (10)

As for eminent descendants, it is enough for us to

mention the prestigious name of Alexander Vachon, born at Saint-Raymond-de-Portneuf on 16 August 1886, from the marriage of J. Alexander Vachon and of Marie Davidson. He was a Laureate of Harvard University, a renowned chemist, the Rector of Laval University, Archbishop of Ottawa, and organizer of the famous Marian Congress of 1948.

In the year 1981 the Diocese of Quebec received a new Archbishop, His Excellency Monseigneur Louis-Albert Vachon, born at Saint-Frederic de Beauce on 4 February 1912. Son of Napoleon Vachon and of Alexandrine Gilbert, he is of the 9th generation. Professor of Philosophy and Theology at Laval University, Superior of the Grand Seminary, Rector of the University of Laval, Auxiliary to His Eminence Maurice Roy in 1977; such are the important qualifications that he brings to Quebec, the oldest Episcopal See in North America, except for that of Mexico.

THE EPIDEMICS

If the "Spanish grippe" left a sad souvenir among our ancestors, one could say that the medicine of 1700 was even more useless in the face of those epidemics, the worst of all sorts.

Between 1699 and 1703, the Vachon family was hit full force with the mortality of man. Noel Vachon, the husband of Monique Giroux, father of a fruitful son, died at the hospital of Quebec in the midst of the beautiful summer of 1699. The 28th of February 1702, Guillaume Vachon, a 20 year old bachelor was buried at Beauport. Then, in 1703 there were four burials: Pierre on 17 January; M. Madeleine on 18 February; Marguerite, the eldest of the girls, on 24 June. We have to add with sadness that on the next day 25 June, Our Ancestor Paul Vachon, widower of Marguerite Langlois since 25 September 1697, died in his turn after having seen three of his children put in their graves. One might well ask, "What was this terrible sickness that in the single year of 1703, in the space of 6 months, decimated this family?"

The chronicles of the Ursulines provide us with the opportunity to do the precise research necessary to understand the history of these plagues. "In the winter of 1700-1701, there was an illness among the people of Quebec which had some strange symptoms. The sickness came on with a bad cold, soon augmented by a high fever followed by pains in the sides, after which it carried the people away in a few days . . ." M. de Bernieres, doyen of the Cathederal Choir died on 4 December 1700. "By the end of November (1702-03), the sickness began in the city. It had been brought here by a savage from the frontier. It was a kind of measles, accompanied by facial marks, and in less than two months, more than 1500 were ill and between 300 and 400 died." (11) It seems that this epidemic struck down a fourth of the population of Quebec.

There is not any doubt that the last four victims of the Vachon family, including Our Ancestor himself, were laid low by this species of measles. They say that the following year the same pestilence happened in Louisiana. (12)

Such is, in brief, the beautiful story of Ancestor Paul Vachon and his wife Marguerite Langlois who well might deserve a little monument, or at least a commemorative plaque, somewhere in Beauport.

BIBLIOGRAPHY

(1)	BF	Volume 34, pages 272 - 273
(2)	V	Volume II, pages 667 - 668
(3)	BT	Volume I, page 564
(4)	CQ	Pages 12, 13, 29, 79, 363 and 365
(5)	CB & CD	14 September, 1658 and 21 November 1679
(6)	CB	Volume II, Pages 6 - 89
(7)	DI	Pages 13 and 22
(8)	X	Pages 1921 - 1923
(9)	DG	Pages 95, 544, passim
(10)	CZ	Volume 7, page 598
(11)	BH	Volume 2, pages 13 - 15
(12)	CX	Volume 6, page 24, note 3
	CB & H	29 September 1654
	CB & F	21 May 1687
	CB & AD	13 July 1682 and 4 April 1684
	BT	Volumes I, II, III, IV, V, VI, passim.

Nicolas Veilleux

Chapter 26

Nicolas Veilleux

$\mathcal{N}$icolas Veilleux, sailor, son and heir of Nicolas and Perrette Roussel, was originally from Saint-Jacques of Dieppe in Normandy. He wrote his name "Nicolas Verieul."

On 17 July 1694 the Anglo-Dutch fleet destroyed nearly all of the town of Dieppe. That most beautiful church, Saint-Jacques, where Our Ancestor worshipped, was spared. Nevertheless, the record of baptism of Nicolas has never been found. However those of two sisters and a brother have been located in the parish register, as follows: Catherine Vidieu, baptized 16 September 1638; Marie Verdrieul, baptized 25 April 1642; and Thomas Verdrieul, baptized 25 October 1640; all children of Nicolas and of Pierrette Roussel. (1)

THE SAILOR

We find that Nicolas Veilleux must have arrived in Canada in 1658, because on 25 April 1659, before any ships had yet arrived for that year, he signed on as a sailor in the service of Pierre Emouys, Sieur de Saint-Jacques, owner of a boat acquired from Julien Fortin. The contract of employment was made at Quebec before Notary J.B. Peuvret and witnessed by Vincent Poirier and Thierry Delettre. He was to receive a salary of 27 livres a month for four months work. (2)

The next day he sailed with the rest of the crew. They were probably busy hauling cargo up and down the Saint Lawrence River, up until September.

RICHARD AND NICOLAS

The friendship that held Nicolas and Richard Dumesnil together was like that of David and Jonathan of the Bible.

The 29 year old Richard and the 26 year old Nicolas were both Normans, both had been confirmed by Mgr de Laval on 2 February 1660 at Chateau-Richer and both cultivated two farms together, 18 arpents distant from the west coast of the great river, at Sainte-Anne-de-Beaupre. A lease signed between Jean Lepicard and Jean Boutin indicated their mutual presence on the Beaupre coast on 18 July 1660. (3)

On 15 April 1663, according to the last reckoning of la Toussaint (1662), the two farmers leased the most easterly situated part of their land to Isaac Lemy for two years. This land consisted of 3 arpents on the river by 126 arpents in depth. It had been bought from Louis Gagne junior for the price of 136 livres. (4)

A ROYAL GIFT

Nicolas loved Sainte Anne. The proof is abundant. Here is one: in March 1660, Nicolas Veilleux gave 60 livres to the chapel named Sainte-Anne "accepted for the chapel by Sieur Etienne de Lessard, donator of the land for the chapel." (6) This sum was due him from Marin Nourrice; Nourrice himself had a debt to collect from Claude Bouchard of this amount according to a writ of 2 January 1660, made before witnesses Richard Dumesnil and Picard. (7)

It truly was a royal gift, because it helped build the second church of Sainte-Anne, finished in 1661. Nicolas made other gifts, somewhat more modest: 4 livres in 1663, 1 livre in 1666, a bushel of wheat in 1673, etc. (8)

NOSTALGIA

Did our Norman suffer from boredom? Or did he leave to take care of some business? Who knows!

On 26 June 1660, (9) Nicolas "on the eve of his departure for France" ceded to Richard Dumesnil "that portion of grain coming to him from the concession of the widow bacon." Marie Tavernier, widow of Eustace Bacon, had a farm at Chateau-Richer. With the money obtained from this, Richard sent to "Madame sevestre thirty two livres ten sols and to Antoine francois dit le gascon thirty three livres."

On 18 May 1662, Nicolas made "Squire Mathieu d'Amours, Sieur des Chaufour" his general agent, especially to give him the right to receive from G. Moyneau the 27 livres due him on 28 November 1661; and also the 29 livres due from Henry Brauz. (10)

In August Nicolas Chavigneau confessed to "owing a just and honest debt to Nicolas Voidiou (Verieul) in the sum of forty livres for impending bills made to his creditors in order to carry on his urgent business." (11)

THE MARRIAGE

Nicolas Veilleux made a marriage contract with Marguerite Hyardin on Monday, 5 October 1665, at Quebec, before Notary Claude Auber. Present were Julien Fortin, friend Richard Dumesnil, now a Squire, the Intendant Jean Talon, Claude Bouchard, Nicolas Godbout, etc. The future spouse said that she was the daughter of Rene and of Jeanne Serre, of the parish of Saint-Sulpice in Paris. It was learned later that she had a sister Marguerite Yardin, daughter of Rene and of Jeanne Sarrey, born at Jouinville, Haute-Marne, on 30 August 1645. The marriage contract summed up with the notation that whoever died last inherited the estate of the other. (12)

Father Thomas Morel blessed the marriage the following December at Cap Tourmente "in the home of Julien Fortin instead of the church." The act was recorded at Chateau-Richer by this itinerant pastor and reiterated that Nicolas was a sailor by occupation and Marguerite "native of Louenville in Champagne, Parish of Notre Dame." (13) The author lists Marguerite among the King's Daughters. (14)

A FRIENDLY SEPARATION

The two associates decided to sever their mutual affairs. A verbal accord made on 6 January 1666, was ratified before the Notary Auber on the following April third. (15)

Richard Dumesnil became the sole owner of the concession "between Barette and the heirs of the late Guimont," and Nicolas of that "between leVeau and Picard." The farm that Nicolas occupied is today in the center of the town of Beaupre. Since his land was not as well cleared as that of Richard, the latter promised to give "the number of 4 arpents in recompense . . . which 4 arpents will be made ready for planting . . ."

In 1667 Nicolas owned 8 arpents of usable land and employed a hired hand, Jean de la Fond.

Alas! Friend Richard passed away prematurely at Chateau-Richer, at the mill of Sault-a-la-Puce. His burial was on 12 August 1679 at Chateau-Richer.

PAPA AND MAMA

Nicolas and Marguerite had 9 children: 5 girls and 4 boys, of whom 3 died young. Nicolas junior and Joseph were fruitful and assured the perpetuation of the Veilleux family.

Nicolas, the eldest, had his baptismal act recorded at Chateau-Richer in 1667; Marguerite was baptized by Father Fillon on 15 September 1671 at Sainte-Anne; Angelique at Quebec; Marie at Sainte-Famille, I.O.; all the others at Saint-Francois, I.O. In the beginning, the missionaries recorded the acts where and when they had the time to do so. (16)

THE FAMILY MOVES

One day Nicolas decided to go to live on the Ile of Orleans. On 6 March 1676, he acquired a property from

Pierre Gagnon of Chateau-Richer, of 3 arpents of frontage, in exchange for his property at Sainte-Anne. The very next day, he ceded 2 arpents to Jacques Cloutier junior. Then, on 2 March he sold the other arpent to Jean Gagnon. (17)

Was it because of these transactions that the family left the Beaupre coast? It is certain that in 1681 Nicolas owned a site of 5.8 arpents of frontage between Rene Emond and Michel Jenouzeau, on the north coast of the island in Saint Francois parish. There the census taker found he and his family: Nicolas had a hired hand, Michel, 1 gun, and 6 arpents of cleared land. (18) On 20 March 1697, Notary Jacob signed an act wherein it is written that Nicolas and his wife ceded a piece of land of 3 arpents and a house to Jacques Baudon, their son-in-law. Nicolas and Marguerite would hold onto 2.8 arpents, the piece to the west. (19) On 28 March 1708, Nicolas Verieul, age 75, and Marguerite Hyardin gave their estate of 2.8 arpents, situated between Jacques Baudon and the heirs of Etienne Mesny, to their 26 year old son Joseph. (20)

Nicolas Verieul lived to be 80 years old. Then he was interred at Saint-Francois I.O., on 11 October 1714. Marguerite died 6 years later at the same place. Their surviving children were all married. In 1720, Marguerite, Angelique, Marie and Madeleine had married Hypolyte Lehoux, Claude Landry, Antoine Dandurand and Pierre Fougere, respectively. The two boys, Nicolas and Joseph, kept the family name alive. The first married Marie-Anne Mesny and Anne-Madeleine Duchesne. He was the father of 11 children. As for Joseph, he married Marguerite Butant on 30 June 1710. He raised a family of 7 boys and 2 girls.

Honor to those who have fought for their country! Give homage to their spirit of initiative, to their profound faith!

BIBLIOGRAPHY

(1)	DL	Varieur, Wilfred E. Personal Research
(2)	CB & BW	25 April 1659
(3)	CE	Volume 51, pages 124 - 125
(4)	CB & H	25 April 1663
(5)	CB & F	19 April 1664
(6)	CB & F	18 March 1660
(7)	D	PA-16, 4411, pages 4 & 6
(8)	D	973 - 2, page 85
(9)	CB & F	26 June 1660
(10)	CB & H	18 May 1662
(11)	CB & H	11 August 1662
(12)	CB & F	5 October 1665
(13)	CF	Volume I, December 1665
(14)	Y	Pages 260 - 261
(15)	CB & F	3 April 1666
(16)	AG	Pages 33, 55 - 56, 79, 100, 106, 137, 145 - 147
(17)	CB & K	22 March 1676
(18)	AY	Page 275
(19)	CB & AS	20 March 1697
(20)	CB & AS	27 March 1708
	CB & K	14 July 1672 and 22 March 1676
	CB & P	11 November 1694 and 9 November 1713
	CB & Z	11 March 1684
	CB & AD	24 March 1664
	CB & AH	3 February 1685 and 11 October 1693
	CB & D	22 March 1667, 6 March 1683
		30 July 1683, 27 October 1684,
		6 November 1686, 10 June 1688
		20 June 1688, 26 September 1688
	CX1	Pages 212 - 215
	BM	Volume 29, pages 182 - 183

A LIST OF REFERENCES
KEYED TO THE BIBLIOGRAPHIES

A. Adhemar, Antoine. Greffes. Montreal (1668 - 1714), Vol. V, pages 3 - 334. Vol. VI, pages 3 - 312. Trois-Rivieres (1674 - 1699), Vol. XXVII, page 271. Refer CB.

B. Ameau, Severin. Greffes, Trois-Rivieres, First Part (1651-1690), Vol. XI, pages 49-164. Second Part (1690-1702), Vol. XXVI, pages 11 - 33. Refer CB.

C. _____. Saint Anne de Beaupre. Annals. Levis, P.Q. Canada. 1910. Refer CE.

D. _____. Archives, Basilica of Saint Anne, Saint Anne de Beaupre, P.Q. Canada. Various Manuscripts. Refer CE.

E. _____. Archives, Seminary of Quebec, Quebec City, P.Q. Canada. Refer CE.

F. Auber, Claude. Greffes. Quebec (1652 - 1693), Vol. I, pages 115 - 149. Refer CB.

G. Audet, Francis J., S.R.C., La Famille Audet-Lapointe, 30 pages privately printed, 1924.

H. Audouart, Guillaume. Greffes. Quebec (1647 - 1663), Vol. I, pages 33 - 115. Refer CB.

I. Baillargeon, Noel. Le Seminaire de Quebec sous l'Episcopat de Mgr de Laval. 1972.

J. Basset, Benigne. Greffes. Montreal (1657 - 1699), Vol. I, pages 161 - 322. Refer CB.

K. Becquet, Romain. Greffes. Quebec (1663 - 1682), Vol. II, pages 252 - 279. Vol. III, pages 3 - 195. Refer CB.

L. Bellemare, J.E. Histoire de Nicolet. 1923.

M. Bourgine, Hilaire. Greffes. Montreal (1685 - 1690), Vol. XI, pages 5 - 46. Refer CB.

N. Careless, J.M.S. Canada-A Story of Challenge. Toronto: Macmillan of Canada, A Division of Gage Publications, Limited. 1958. pages 59 - 61. Reprinted with permission of the author and publisher.

O. Casgrain, Abbe. Une Paroisse Canadienne. 1880.

P.   Chambelon, Louis. Greffes. Quebec (1692 - 1702), Vol. XVIII. Refer CB.

Q.   _____. Collection de Pieces Judiciaries et Notariales, premiere liasse (No 70). Refer BT.

R.   Costain, Thomas B. The White and the Gold: The French Regime in Canada. New York Doubleday & Company, Inc.

S.   Courteau, Elmer. The King's Daughters. Sparta, WI: Reisinger, privately printed, ca. 1980. Reprinted from a nine part series published in Lost in Canada? from 2:2 (April 1976) to 4:2 (April 1978).

T.   Dauzet, Albert. Dictionnaire Eytmologique des Noms de Famille et Prenoms de France. Paris: Librairie Larousse, 1951.

U.   Deziel, Julien, and collaborators. Medaillons d'Ancetres. 2 Vols., Montreal: Editions Paulines, 1970 - 1973.

V.   _____. Dictionary of Canadian Biography. Toronto: University of Toronto Press: Vols I to XI, 1981.

W.   Dionne, N.E. Galerie Historique. 1910.

X.   Drouin, Gabriel. Dictionnaire National des Canadiens Francais (1608 - 1760). Montreal: Institut Genealogique Drouin, 1965; rev. ed., 1975.

Y.   Dumas, Sylvio. Les Filles du Roi en Nouvelle-France. Quebec: Societe Historique de Quebec, pub. No 24, 1972.

Z.   Duquet, Pierre. Greffes. Quebec (1663 - 1687), Vol. II, pages 109 - 248. Refer CB.

AA. Faillon, Etienne Michel. Histoire de la Colonie Francaise en Canada. Montreal: 3 Volumes, 1865.

AB. Falardeau, Etienne. Les Pionniers de Longueuil, 1937.

AC. Faucher-Asselin, Jacqueline. Les Asselin, Histoire et Diction-naire Genealogique des Asselin en Amerique. 1981.

AD. Fillon, Michel. Greffes. Quebec (1660 - 1688), Vol. II, pages 94 - 109. Refer CB.

AE. Fortin, Cora. Premier Fortin d'Amerique, Julien Fortin. Cahier Special F, Societe de Genealogie de Quebec, 1974.

AF. Fortin, J.-Henri, De France au Canada, Charles Fortin. Manuscript printed privately. 1973.

AF1. Gagne, Lucien and Asselin, Jean-Pierre, C.Ss.R. Saint Anne de Beaupre, Pilgrim's Goal for Three Hundred Years. A brief history of the Shrine. Second Edition: 1971.

AG. Gariepy, Raymond. Les Seigneuries de Beaupre et de l'Ile d'Orleans dans leur debuts. Cahiers d'Histoire No 27, Quebec: La Societe Historique de Quebec, 1974.

AH. Genaple, Francois. Greffes. Quebec (1682 - 1709), Vol. VII, pages 1 - 192. Refer CB.

AI. Godbout, Archange. Emigration Rochelaise en Nouvelle-France. Reprint edition with corrections and additions by Roland-J. Auger; Montreal: Editions Elysee, 1980. Reprinted from "Familles Venues de La Rochelle en Canada." Rapport des Archives Nationales du Quebec (1970): pages 113 - 367.

AJ. Godbout, Archange. Les Passagers du St-Andre. Montreal: Societe Genealogique Canadienne-Francaise 1964.

AK. Godbout, Archange. "Nos Ancetres aux XVIIe Siecle: Dictionnaire Genealogique et Bio-Bibliographique des Familles Canadiennes." Rapport des Archives Nationales du Quebec. Refer CE.

AK1.Godbout, Archange. Origines des Familles Canadiennes-Francaises, 1925.

AL. Gourdeau de Beaulieu, Jacques. Greffes. Quebec (1662 - 1663), Vol. II, page 91. Refer CB.

AM. Gregoire, Jeanne. La Source et la Filon. Privately printed. 1961.

AN. Gregoire, Jeanne. Le Dict de Gregoire de Blois. Privately printed. 1962.

AO. Hollier, Robert. La France des Canadiens. 1962.

AP. Hudon, Pierre-Henri. Riviere-Ouelle de la Bouteillerie. 1972.

AQ. _____. Inventaire des Insinuations de la Prevote de Quebec. 3 Volumes, Quebec: Archives de la Province du Quebec, 1939. Refer CE.

AR. _____. Inventaire des Ordonnance des intendants de la Nouvelle-France Conserves aux Archives Provinciales de Quebec. 4 Vols., Beauceville: L'Eclaireur, Ltee., 1919.

AS. Jacob, Etienne. Greffes. Quebec (1680 - 1726), Vol. VII, pages 193 - 300. Refer CB.

AT. Janneau, Etienne. Greffes. Quebec (1691 - 1743), Vol. XIV, pages 7 - 104. Refer CB.

AU. Jobin and Vincent. Histoire de Longueuil et de la Famille de Longueuil. Privately printed. 1889.

AV. _____. Journal des Jesuits, edited by Laverdiere and Casgrain, Montreal. 1892.

AW. Juchereau and Duplessis. Les Annales de l'Hotel Dieu de Quebec. 1939.

AX. Laberge, Lionel. Histoire du Fief de Lotinville 1652 - 1690. L'Ange-Gardien. 1963.

AY. Lafontaine, Andre. Recensement annote de la Nouvelle-France 1681.

AY1._____. L'Ancetre, Societe de Genealogie de Quebec, C.P. 2234 Quebec, P.Q. Canada, G1K 7N8, 1974.

AZ. Leblond de Brumath, A. L'Histoire Populaire de Montreal. 1926.

BA. Leboeuf, J. Arthur. Complement au Dictionnaire Genelogique Tanguay. 2 Volumes in 1. Montreal: Societe Genealogique Canadienne-Francaise, 1977.

BB. Lecoustre, Claude. Greffes. Quebec (1647-1648), Vol. I pages 24 - 28. Refer CB.

BC. Le Jeune, L., Dictionnaire General du Canada. 1931.

BD. Lepallieur, Francois. Greffes. Montreal (1733 - 1739), Vol. XXV. Refer CB.

BE. _____. Les Anciennes Familles du Quebec. Compiled originally for La Brasserie Labatt Limitee, Lachine, Quebec. Many of the portraits of Our Ancestors in this book have been reprinted from this charming set of charcoal drawings, with the kind permission of the Labatt Breweries.

BF. _____. Les Bulletin des Recherches Historiques, now defunct (1895 - 1968, 70 Volumes). See Pierre-Georges Roy, Index du Bulletin des Recherches Historiques, Organe du Bureau des Archives 1895 - 1925 (4 Volumes, Beauceville: L'Eclaireur, Ltee., 1925 - 1926).

BG. _____. Les Cahiers des Dix. Les Societe des Dix, c/o Librairie Garneau. Ltee., 333 Ouest, 55e Rue, C.P. 7600, Charlesbourg, P.Q. Canada, G1G 5W7 (1936).

BH. _____. Les Ursulines de Quebec. 1864.

BI. Le Tenneur, Rene. Les Normands et les Origines du Canada Francais. 1970.

BJ. _____. Livre-Souvenir de la Famille Blanchet. Privately printed. 1946.

BK. Maugue, Claude. Greffes. Montreal (1674 - 1696), Vol. IX pages 5 - 328. Refer CB.

BL. Michon, Abel. Greffes. Quebec (1709 - 1749), Vol. XXII. Refer CB.

BM. _____. Memoires, Societe Genealogique Canadienne-Francaise, C.P. 335, Station Place d'Armes, Montreal, P.Q., Canada, H2Y 3H1 (1944). Cumulative Indexes: vols. 1 - 16 in 17:2 (April - June 1966): 116 - 128; vols. 1 - 20 in 22:4 (October - December 1970): 218 - 236; and vols. 21 - 31 in 31:4 (October - December 1980): 295 - 317.

BN. Marquis, Charles-Eugene. Nos Fortin. Dans la Revue Paroissiale de Sainte-Anne-de-Beaupre, MON CLOCHER, 1964 pages 38 - 40.

BO. Massicotte, Edouard-Zotique. Faits Curieux de l'Histoire de Montreal. 1924.

BP. Massicotte, Edouard-Zotique. "Les Colons de Montreal de 1642 a 1667." Memoires de la Societe Royale du Canada. 1913, 3rd series, vol. 7, in Les Bulletin des Recherches Historique from 33:3 (March 1927) to 33:11 (November 1927) with additions and corrections in 37:12 (December 1931): 757 - 759.

BQ. Montagne, Mme. Pierre. Tourouvre et les Juchereau: Un Chapitre de l'Emigration Percheronne au Canada. Quebec: Societe Canadienne de Genealogie, 1965.

BR. Mouchy, Nicolas de. Greffes. Quebec and Montreal (1664 - 1667) Vol. II, pages 249 - 252. Refer CB.

BS. Nadeau, Eugene. Mere Leonie. Fides, 1950.

BT. _____. New France, Conseil Souverain (ou Superior). Jugements et Deliberations du Conseil Souverain (ou Superior) de la Nouvelle-France (1663 - 1716). 6 vols., in 12, Quebec: Imprimerie Joseph Dussault, 1885 - 1891.

BU. _____. Nos Racines: L'Histoire Vivante des Quebecois. 395 Boul., Lebeau, Saint-Laurent, P.Q. Canada. H4N 1S2.

BV. _____. Ordonnances, Commissions, Etc., Etc., des Gouverneurs et Intendants de la Nouvelle-France. 1639 - 1706. 2 Vols., Beauceville: L'Eclaireur, Ltee. 1924.

BV0. Paquin, Frere Pasteur. Petite Histoire des Familles Paquin en Amerique 1672 - 1976. Les Editions Etchemin. 241 pages. 1976.

BV1. Parent, Anne-Marie. Notre Pierre et nos autres Aieux. 1968. Privately printed manuscript.

BW. Peuvret de Mesnu, Jean-Baptiste. Greffes. Quebec (1653 - 1659) Vol. II, pages 1 - 6. Refer CB.

BX. Pilote, Abbe Georges-Renaud. Cure de Colbeau, P.Q. Canada. Custodian of the research of Sister Gerardine I. Pilote.

BZ. Pottier, Jean-Baptiste. Greffes. Montreal and Trois-Rivieres (1686 - 1711), Vol. XI, pages 167 - 258. Refer CB.

CA. _____. Public Archives of Canada, Manuscript Division. General Inventory of Manuscripts. 7 Volumes. Ottawa: Information Canada 1971 - 1977. Covers manuscript groups 1 - 27, 29 and 30.

CB. Quebec, Archives Nationales du Quebec. Inventaire des Greffes des Notaires du Regime Francais. 27 vols., Quebec: Roch Lefebvre, 1942 - 1976. A separate index for vols. I through VIII was published in 1974.

CC. Quebec, District Judiciare de Montreal. "Contrats de Mariage, 1650 - 1839." Public Archives of Canada, MG 8 (C 4). An alphebetical index of the marriage contracts of Montreal containing the names of the engaged couple, the notary, and the date of the act. A similar index exists at the Archives Nationales du Quebec and was created by Edouard-Zotique Massicotte, Inventaire des Contrats de Mariage Conserves aux Archives Judiciares de Montreal. 12 Volumes.

CD. Rageot, Gilles. Greffes. Quebec (1666 - 1692), Vol. III, pages 197 - 300, and Vol. IV, pages 3 - 254. Refer CB.

CE. Quebec, Archives Nationales du Quebec. Rapport des Archives Nationales du Quebec. (formerly called Rapport de l'Archiviste de la Province de Quebec and Rapport des Archives du Quebec). For an index see Quebec, Ministere des Affaires Culturelles, Table des Matieres des Rapport des Archives du Quebec, Tomes 1 a 42 (1920 - 1964). Quebec: Roch Lefebvre. 1965.

CE1. Raimbault, Joseph-Charles. Greffes. Montreal. Volume XXI pages 1 - 228. Refer CB.

CF. _____. Registre de la Paroisse de Chateau-Richer, Quebec. Refer CE.

CG. _____. Registres de la Paroisse de Trois-Rivieres, Quebec. Refer CE.

CH. _____. Registres de la Paroisse de Quebec City, Quebec. Refer CE.

CI. _____. Registres de la Paroisse de Sainte-Anne-de-Beaupre, Quebec. Refer CE.

CJ. _____. Revue d'Histoire de l'Amerique Francaise. L'Institut d'Histoire de l'Amerique Francaise, 261, ave. Bloomfield, Outremont, Montreal, Quebec H2V 3R6 (1947). Vols. XI-XX, 1957-1967; and Vols. XXI-XXX, 1967 - 1977.

CK. _____. Saint Anne de Beaupre. Revue. Published monthly by the Redemptorist Fathers. Printed in Canada. CP 1000 Sainte Anne de Beaupre, P.Q. Canada G0A 3C0.

CL. Rheaume, Joseph (Frere Joseph, O.F.M.), 2010, boulevard Dorchester Ouest, Montreal, P.Q. Canada H3H 1R6. Brother Joseph is the inheritor and custodian of all the documentation on the Rheaume family that was collected by the Abbot Anselme Rheaume.

CM. Rock, Lucille Fournier. Our French-Canadian Forefathers. Woonsocket, R.I.: Rock Publications, 1982.

CN. Roy, Antoine, ed. "Bibliographie de Genealogies et Histoires de Familles." Rapport des Archives Nationales du Quebec (1940 - 41).

CO. Roy, Joseph Edmond. Guillaume Couture Primier Colon de la Pointe Levy, Levis, P.Q. Canada 1884, Mercier & Cie. Libraires Imprimeurs.

CO1.Roy, Joseph Edmond. Nicolas Leroy et ses Descendants (1897), 255 pages.

CP. Roy, Joseph Edmond. La Seigneurie de Lauzon. 1897.

CQ. Roy, Leon. Les Terres de l'Ile de Orleans. Montreal: Editions Bergeron, 1978. Reprinted from the Rapport des Archives du Quebec (1949/50 - 1950/51): 149 - 260, (1951/52 - 1952/53): 303 - 368, (1953/54 - 1954/55): 3 - 69, and (1973): 115 - 237.

CR. Roy, Pierre-Georges. Atravers l'Histoire de Beaumont. 1943.

CS. Roy, Pierre-Georges. Inventaire des Contrats de Mariage du Regime Francais Conserves aux Archives Judiciares de Quebec. 6 Volumes, Quebec: Archives de la Province du Quebec. 1937 - 1938.

CT. Roy, Pierre-Georges. Les Juges de la Province de Quebec. 1933.

CU. Roy, Pierre-Georges. Papier-Terrier (1667 - 1668).

CV. Seguin, Robert-Lionel. La Vie Libertine en Nouvelle-France au dix-septieme siecle (1972).

CW. _____. Societe Historique du Nouvel-Ontario. Documents Historique No 19. 1950.

CX. Sulte, Benjamin. Histoire des Canadiens-Francaise, 1608 - 1880. 8 Volumes. Montreal: Wilson & Co., 1882 - 1884.

CX1.Talbot, Eloi-Gerard. Genealogie des Familles Originaires des Comtes de Montmagny l'Islet Bellechasse. 1976.

CY. Talbot, Eloi-Gerard. Inventaire des Contrats de Mariages au greffe de Charlevoix. 1943.

CZ. Tanguay, Cyprian. Dictionnaire Genealogique des Familles Canadiennes. 7 volumes. Montreal: Eusabe Senecal, 1871 - 1890; reprinted., Montreal: Editions Elysee, 1975 and Pawtucket, R.I. 1982. Quintin-Rock Pubs.

DA. Tanguay, Cyprian. Repertoire General du Clerge Canadien. 1893.

DB. Thwaites, Reuben G., ed. The Jesuit Relations and Allied Documents (1610 - 1791). 73 Volumes in 36. New York: Pegeant Books Co., 1959.

DC. Tremblay, Jean-Paul. Le Perche des Aieux. 1979.

DE. Trudel, Marcel. Atlas Historique du Canada Francais des Origines a 1867. Quebec: Les Presses de l'Universite Laval. 1961. Also see Trudel's revised An Atlas of New France. 2nd ed., Quebec: Les Presses de l'Universite Laval, 1973.

DF. Trudel, Marcel. Initiation a la Nouvelle-France, histoire et institutions. Montreal/Toronto: Holt Rinehart Winston, Ltd. 1968.

DG. Trudel, Marcel. Le Terrier du Saint-Laurent en 1663. Ottawa: Editions de l'Universite d'Ottawa. 1973.

DH. Turcotte, L.-P. l'Ile d'Orleans. 1867.

DI. Vachon, Andre. Histoire du Notariat Canadien. 1962.

DJ. Vachon, Andre. "Inventaire Critique des Notaries Royaux des Gouvernements de Quebec, Montreal et Trois-Rivieres (1663 - 1764)." Revue d'Histoire de l'Amerique Francaise. An eight part series printed form 9:3 (December 1955) to 11:3 (December 1957)

DK. Vachon, Paul. Greffes. Quebec (1658 - 1693), Volume II, pages 6 - 89. Refer CB.

DL. Varieur, Wilfred E. P. O. Box 4609, Stamford, CT. 16907 Personal Research in Parish Archives in France. 1980.

APPENDIX A

An English Glossary of Words Found in French-Canadian Genealogy

Every discipline has its jargon, no less does genealogy. However, in researching the original notarial acts of New France, we come across a terminology in which, even if we are able to make the bridge from Old to New French, the exact meaning escapes us.

The reason for this stems from the fact that the colonial origins of French and English America were so different. The colonial Englishman was a freeholder for the most part; a landowning free agent not tied to Church or Crown. The Frenchman transplanted to Canada was, on the other hand, subjected to a feudal system where the authority of Church and State was ever present in his daily life. Thus many words and phrases peculiar to this system are found in the records of Our Ancestors.

This Glossary is provided to help the reader understand these words and phrases, especially if he or she should have the opportunity to delve into the original documents.

Your comments, suggestions for improvement, and/or submission of additional items for inclusion in subsequent volumes of this series would be welcome.

The Author

WORD OR PHRASE	DESCRIPTION
ACQUET	Acquisition of property in common by partners in marriage.
ACTE	An act, an action, a bill, a deed, an indenture or almost any official document.
AFFERMER	Literally, to lease or to rent. In this context however, it signifies an act whereby a father gives his son the family property before his demise.
ARPENT	A unit of measurement commonly found in the records of New France. See Appendix B.
ADVANCE d'HOIRE	An advance on a legacy.
AYANT CAUSE	A person who has acquired a right or an obligation from another, i.e. the recipient or grantee in a contractual arrangement. These are known in English as the "assigns."
BAIL	A lease. There are several kinds of bail: Bail a ferme—a lease on a farm Bail a loyer—a lease on a house Bail emphyteotique—confers the right to lease seizable property. Passer un bail—to sign an agreement or to draw up a lease.
BETES A CORNES	Horned beasts, i.e. cattle.
BIENS	Wealth. Biens immeubles = Real property. Biens meuble = Personal property.

CADASTRE	A duly recorded land survey.
CENS	A seigneurial tax on a tenant, usually levied in kind.
CHELIN	A unit of currency similar to the English shilling, valued at about 20 sous.
CIRCONSTANCES et DEPENDENCES	The right of a relative or a friend to receive a gift from the estate of a deceased person prior to the division of the estate among the heirs.
CONCESSION	A land grant from the King, usually bestowed through one of his representatives, i.e. the Company, the Intendant or the Church.
CONTRAT	A contract, as in modern usage.
CONTRAT de MARIAGE	An agreement prior to a marriage fixing the ownership of spousal property during the marriage.
CONTRAT de VENTE	Deed of sale.
COUTUME de PARIS	A codification of customary law. The law was a compromise between the assumption that an individual had a natural right to the land and the desire to preserve the integrity of the family estate. It involved the manner in which the land was passed on to the heirs.
DENIER	A unit of old money, valued at the 240th part of a livre.
DONATION	A lifetime lease. A contract by which one conveys real estate for a specified time, usually for life, in return for a

	specified performance or rent or both.
ACTE de DONATION	The act of voluntarily abandoning rights in return for advantages.
DONATION entre VIF	The same kind of an act as above, between living persons.
DONATION VIAGRE	The same kind of an act as above, where one retains use of the donation during his or her lifetime.
DOUAIRE	Customary right of the surviving spouse to the property of the other.
DOT	The dowry a wife brings to the marriage reckoned in money, property or other material wealth.
FABRIQUE	The manner of administering the churches of Quebec. In the other provinces of Canada, like in the USA, the Bishop is responsible for civil administration through a Chancery Office. Historically, in Quebec, the parish church preceded the diocese and organized a "fabrique" of "marguilliers" for this purpose.
FEU et LIEU	Literally, fire and place, meaning the family hearth. Used when counting domiciles or as an alternate word for home.
FIANCAILLES	A promise of marriage made by the engaged couple before a priest. This word is always found in the plural.
FIEF	A feudal estate. The lord gives the use of a piece of his land to a serf in return for certain services fixed by custom. A modified form of this system determined the land use in

New France between the habitant and his seigneur.

HOIRS — Heirs, as in the phrase "lui, ses hoirs et ayant cause," meaning "him, his heirs and assigns." The word "heritiers" has largely supplanted the old "hoirs."

GREFFES — Registry records maintained by a Notary, or "Greffier," who may be a court clerk, a recorder or a registrar.

HONORABLE — A title adopted by middle class gentry who, although not of the nobility, wished to distinguish themselves from the peasants who were known as "habitants." It was a title implying dignity and esteem. Usually used by merchants who could read and write, therefore genteel.

HUISSIER — An official enforcer, usually a sheriff, bailiff or process server.

HUISSIER AUDIENCIER — A court crier.

HYPOTHEQUE — Mortgage. To "purge un hypotheque" is to pay off the mortgage.

INDIVIS — Indivisable. Refers to something of value when used in a contract, i.e. a piece of real estate or personal property in which many people have an interest and which cannot be materially divided between them. For example, if 3 people own a rare painting, the wealth is divisable, the property is not.

INTERDIT — To forbid, prohibit or deprive of civil rights.

INVENTAIRE	Inventory, both noun and verb. It describes the act of listing, describing and evaluating in writing, the elements of ownership of a person, a community, or of an inheritance. It includes all papers as well as debts and contracts.
LEGATAIRE	Legatee or inheritor.
LIEUE	League, a unit of measurement. See Appendix B.
LIVRE	Similar to an English pound as a unit of currency. Originally equal to one pound of silver.
LOUIS	A former gold piece stamped with the image of the King, hence "Louis." Originally had a value equal to 10 silver livres.
LODS	An act of approval. Consent given by the seigneur to an exchange of property.
LODS et VENTS	The right to divide up land between buyer and seller, as perceived and approved by the seigneur, in order to ensure payment of the "Cens."
MAINTENUE	Confirmation of possession.
MARGUILLIERS	More than a ceremonial title, these responsible parishioners were in charge of the administration of the revenues and expenditures of the parish. Collectively they were known a "la fabrique de (name of parish)." They usually sat together in a special pew during Holy Mass.
NOTAIRE	Notary. A public officer who writes

and attests to deeds and other public records.

OBLIGATION	An act whereby an individual admits to a debt he must pay, a lein he must satisfy or a performance from him required by law. Also a bond.
ONDOYEE	A baptism in extremis. Usually done by a person other than a priest.
PERCHE	A unit of measurement. See Appendix B.
PIASTRE	A Spanish coin accepted as a medium of exchange.
PIED	A foot. A unit of measurement. See Appendix B.
PRECIPUT	A right accorded to a spouse or an inheritor to preselect items from the personal belongings of the late departed in advance of the division among the heirs.
PRISEE	Establishing the value of something by a commissioned appraiser. May also be the record kept by a justice of the peace.
PROCES VERBAL	An official report made by competent authority which may have juridicial consequences.
PROCURER	The prosecutor. A civil official similar to an attorney-general.
PROCURER FISCAL	The comptroller. A civil official similar to an inspector-general of finance.
QUIT RENT	A fixed rent payable in commutation of certain feudal services.
QUITTANCE	A discharge from a debt or obliga-

tion. A writ in recognition that a debtor has satisfied his obligation. A quit claim.

RANG

A row of something: soldiers, farmhouses along a road, land grants along a river.

REPERTOIRE

A reportory such as a listing, a catalog, a table or an index.

SAISINE

The right of the seigneur to foreclose or repossess land or to attach the personal effects of a person who may have failed to meet the obligations of a concession.

SEIGNEUR

The lord and master in a system of feudal relations.

An honorable title bestowed on persons of high rank.

SEIGNEURY

The land of the seigneur.

Feudal rights that go with the land.

Authority of the lord over the land and the people on it.

SIEUR

A form of address prior to the use of "Monsieur." It was used to address a person who was a landowner but not a "Seigneur."

SOL

Old French unit of currency equal in value to 1/20th of a livre. The forerunner of the "sou."

TESTAMENT

A will. The person who makes the will is the TESTATEUR or TESTATRICE. A will can be handwritten, TESTAMENT OLOGRAPHE; or oral, TESTAMENT ORALE.

TOISE	A unit of measurement. See Appendix B.
TRAIT CARRE	A record which establishes the borders of a property.
TRAIT QUARRE	A square tract of land.
TUTELAIRE	A guardian.
TUTUER SUBROGE	A deputy guardian chosen by a member of the family, to protect the interest of minor children. This person would not be a member of the family, hence "subroge" or deputy.
QUITTANCE d'un TUTELLE	Notification to a guardian that he is no longer responsible for the minor child.
VENTE A REMERE	Sale with power of redemption.
VIDIMER	Certification that a document conforms to the original.

APPENDIX B

Table of Measurements

Lacking any indications to the contrary, the measures given here are the old French measures of length and of surface area: "pied, toise, perche, arpent et lieue". (See Glossary). Conforming to the rules established by the "Cent-Associes", calculations are based on the perche of 18 pieds, on the arpent of 180 pieds, and on the lieue of 84 arpents.

Old French	British/USA	Canadian Metric
Linear measurements		
le pied	1.066 feet	0.325 meters
la toise	6.396 feet	1.95 meters
la perche	19.188 feet	5.85 meters
l'arpent*	192 feet	58.522 meters
la lieue	3.1 miles	4.99 kilometers
Surface measurements		
la pied carree	1.136 sq. feet	0.105 sq. meters
la toise carree	40.96 sq. feet	3.804 sq. meters
la perche carree	368.64 sq. feet	34.25 sq. meters
l'arpent carree	0.846 acres	0.342 hectares
la lieue carree	9.33 miles	2415.63 hectares

*The British/USA mile = 27.5 arpents

APPENDIX C

The Geographic Location
of Parishes and Seigneuries in
New France
from
An Atlas of New France
by
Marcel Trudel
The Presses of Laval University
Quebec 1973

Note: Pages cited above are from the ATLAS, not from this book.

FOREWORD

On the following maps, we have attempted to locate the various seigneuries and parishes, as they were in 1760, by *Gouvernments* or Administrative Districts. We have not included the Gaspe since there were no seigneuries there.

From Mitis to Deschaillons and from Les Grondines to Les Eboulements, both shores of the river had been granted in seigniorial tenure by this date.

Each Administrative District was sub-divided into Parishes; each parish had a Cure as its religious head and a Captain of Militia who was the local authority in civil and military matters.

Marcel Trudel
Doctor of Letters
University of Ottawa

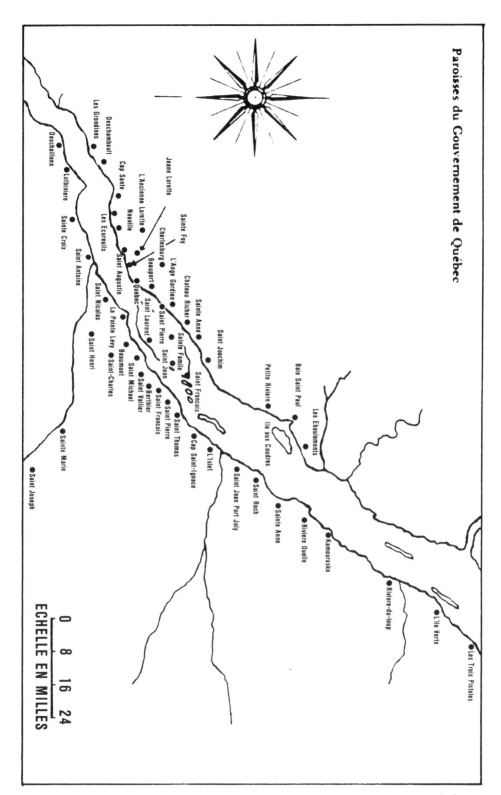

Paroisses du Gouvernement de Québec

ECHELLE EN MILLES

0 8 16 24

C-3

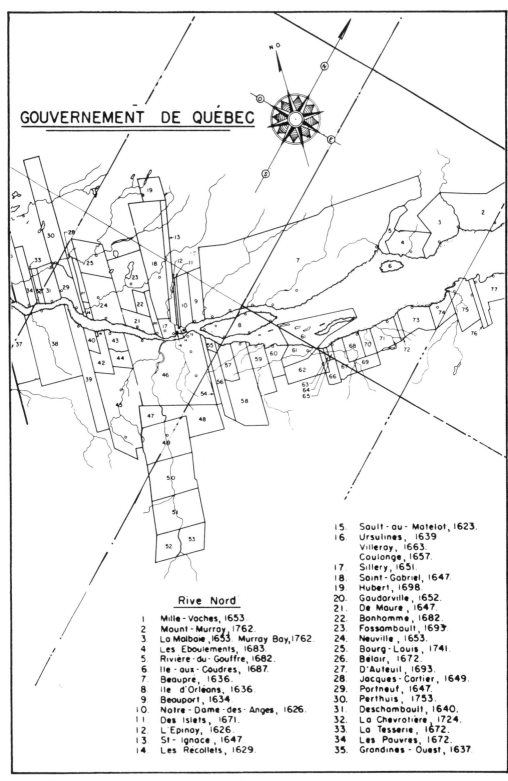

GOUVERNEMENT DE QUÉBEC

Rive Nord

1.	Mille - Vaches, 1653.
2.	Mount - Murray, 1762.
3.	La Malbaie ,1653. Murray Bay,1762.
4.	Les Eboulements, 1683.
5.	Rivière-du- Gouffre, 1682.
6.	Ile - aux - Coudres, 1687.
7.	Beaupre, 1636.
8.	Ile d'Orléans, 1636.
9.	Beauport, 1634.
10.	Notre - Dame -des- Anges, 1626.
11.	Des Islets, 1671.
12.	L'Epinay, 1626.
13.	St- Ignace, 1647.
14.	Les Récollets, 1629.
15.	Sault - au - Matelot, 1623.
16.	Ursulines, 1639
	Villeray, 1663.
	Coulonge, 1657.
17.	Sillery, 1651.
18.	Saint - Gabriel, 1647.
19.	Hubert, 1698.
20.	Gaudarville, 1652.
21.	De Maure, 1647.
22.	Bonhomme, 1682.
23.	Fossambault, 1693.
24.	Neuville, 1653.
25.	Bourg-Louis, 1741.
26.	Belair, 1672.
27.	D'Auteuil, 1693.
28.	Jacques-Cartier, 1649.
29.	Portneuf, 1647.
30.	Perthuis, 1753.
31.	Deschambault, 1640.
32.	La Chevrotière, 1724.
33.	La Tesserie, 1672.
34.	Les Pauvres, 1672.
35.	Grondines - Ouest, 1637.

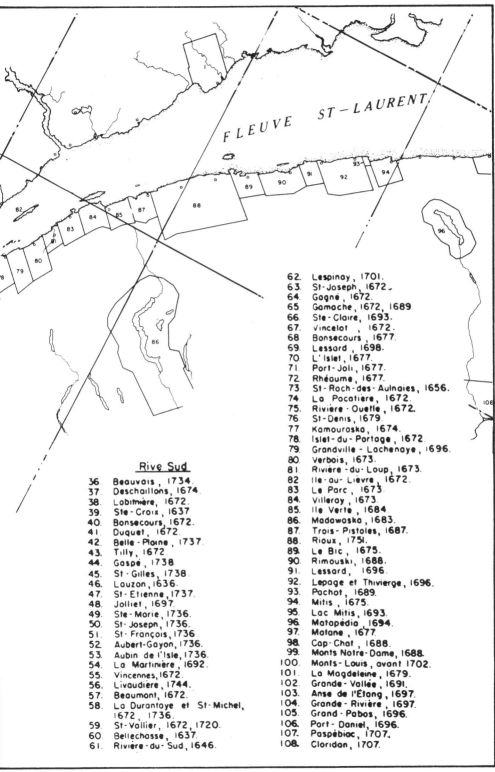

FLEUVE ST - LAURENT

62. Lespinay, 1701.
63. St-Joseph, 1672.
64. Gagné, 1672.
65. Gamache, 1672, 1689.
66. Ste-Claire, 1693.
67. Vincelot, 1672.
68. Bonsecours, 1677.
69. Lessard, 1698.
70. L'Islet, 1677.
71. Port-Joli, 1677.
72. Rhéaume, 1677.
73. St-Roch-des-Aulnaies, 1656.
74. La Pocatière, 1672.
75. Rivière-Ouelle, 1672.
76. St-Denis, 1679.
77. Kamouraska, 1674.
78. Islet-du-Portage, 1672.
79. Grandville-Lachenaye, 1696.
80. Verbois, 1673.
81. Rivière-du-Loup, 1673.
82. Ile-au-Lièvre, 1672.
83. Le Parc, 1673.
84. Villeray, 1673.
85. Ile Verte, 1684.
86. Madawaska, 1683.
87. Trois-Pistoles, 1687.
88. Rioux, 1751.
89. Le Bic, 1675.
90. Rimouski, 1688.
91. Lessard, 1696.
92. Lepage et Thivierge, 1696.
93. Pachot, 1689.
94. Mitis, 1675.
95. Lac Mitis, 1693.
96. Matapédia, 1694.
97. Matane, 1677.
98. Cap-Chat, 1688.
99. Monts Notre-Dame, 1688.
100. Monts-Louis, avant 1702.
101. La Magdeleine, 1679.
102. Grande-Vallée, 1691.
103. Anse de l'Étang, 1697.
104. Grande-Rivière, 1697.
105. Grand-Pabos, 1696.
106. Port-Daniel, 1696.
107. Paspébiac, 1707.
108. Cloridan, 1707.

Rive Sud

36. Beauvais, 1734.
37. Deschaillons, 1674.
38. Lobitmière, 1672.
39. Ste-Croix, 1637.
40. Bonsecours, 1672.
41. Duquet, 1672.
42. Belle-Plaine, 1737.
43. Tilly, 1672.
44. Gaspé, 1738.
45. St-Gilles, 1738.
46. Lauzon, 1636.
47. St-Etienne, 1737.
48. Jolliet, 1697.
49. Ste-Marie, 1736.
50. St-Joseph, 1736.
51. St-François, 1736.
52. Aubert-Gayon, 1736.
53. Aubin de l'Isle, 1736.
54. La Martinière, 1692.
55. Vincennes, 1672.
56. Livaudière, 1744.
57. Beaumont, 1672.
58. La Durantaye et St-Michel, 1672, 1736.
59. St-Vallier, 1672, 1720.
60. Bellechosse, 1637.
61. Rivière-du-Sud, 1646.

C-5

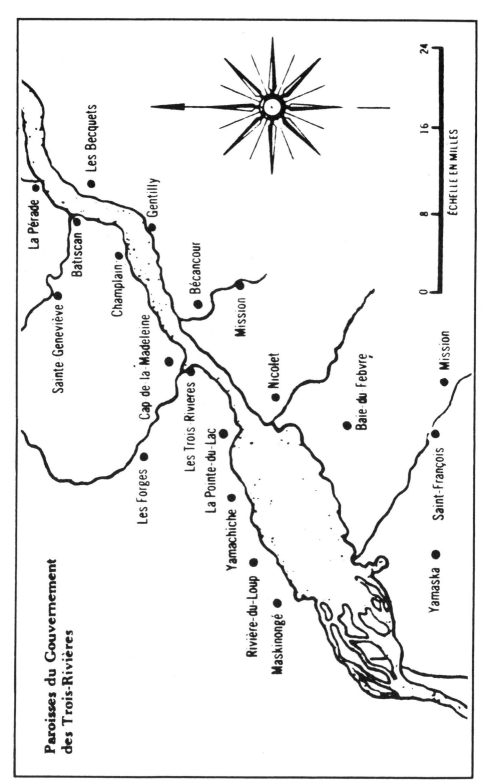

Paroisses du Gouvernement
des Trois-Rivières

ÉCHELLE EN MILLES

0   8   16   24

La Pérade

Les Becquets

Batiscan

Gentilly

Champlain

Sainte-Geneviève

Bécancour

Cap-de-la-Madeleine

Mission

Les Trois-Rivières

Les Forges

Nicolet

La Pointe-du-Lac

Mission

Yamachiche

Baie-du-Febvre

Rivière-du-Loup

Saint-François

Maskinongé

Yamaska

C-6

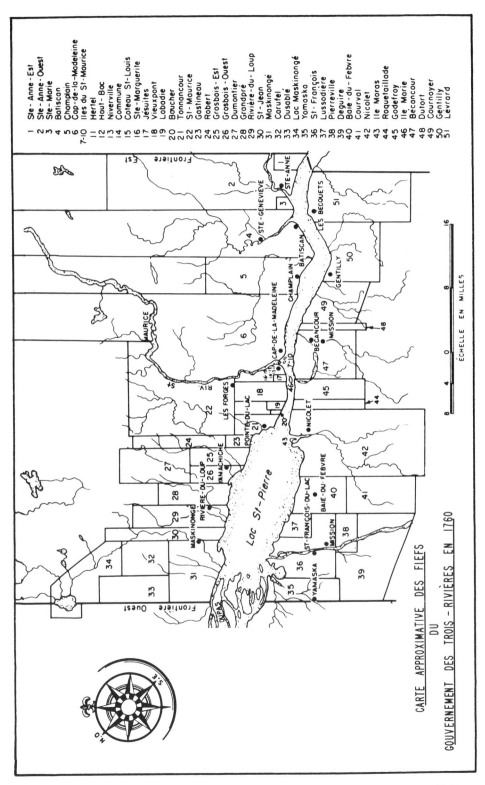

1   Ste - Anne - Est
2   Ste - Anne - Ouest
3   Ste - Marie
4   Batiscan
5   Champlain
6   Cap-de-la-Madeleine
7-10 Iles du St-Maurice
11   Hertel
12   Haut- Boc
13   Niverville
14   Commune
15   Coteau St-Louis
16   Ste-Marguerite
17   Jésuites
18   Vieuxpont
19   Labadie
20   Boucher
21   Tonnancour
22   St - Maurice
23   Gastineau
24   Robert
25   Grosbois - Est
26   Grosbois - Ouest
27   Dumontier
28   Grandpré
29   Rivière-du - Loup
30   St-Jean
31   Maskinongé
32   Carufel
33   Dusablé
34   Lac Maskinongé
35   Yamaska
36   St-François
37   Lussodière
38   Pierreville
39   Deguire
40   Baie-du - Febvre
41   Courval
42   Nicolet
43   Ile Moras
44   Roquetaillade
45   Godefroy
46   Ile Marie
47   Bécancour
48   Dutort
49   Cournoyer
50   Gentilly
51   Lévrard

CARTE APPROXIMATIVE DES FIEFS
DU
GOUVERNEMENT DES TROIS - RIVIÈRES EN 1760

ÉCHELLE EN MILLES

C-7

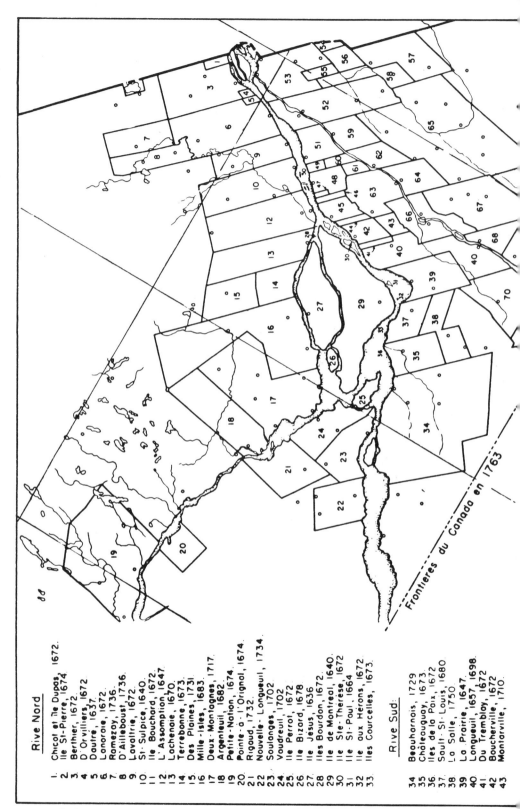

Rive Nord

1. Chicot et Île Dupas, 1672.
2. Île St-Pierre, 1674.
3. Berthier, 1672.
4. D'Orvilliers, 1672.
5. Dautré, 1637.
6. Lanoraie, 1672.
7. Ramezay, 1736.
8. D'Aillebout, 1736.
9. Lavaltrie, 1672.
10. St-Sulpice, 1640.
11. Île Bouchard, 1672.
12. L'Assomption, 1647.
13. Lachenaie, 1670.
14. Terrebonne, 1673.
15. Des Plaines, 1731.
16. Mille-Isles, 1683.
17. Deux-Montagnes, 1717.
18. Argenteuil, 1682.
19. Petite-Nation, 1674.
20. Pointe-à-l'Orignal, 1674.
21. Rigaud, 1732.
22. Nouvelle-Longueuil, 1734.
23. Soulanges, 1702.
24. Vaudreuil, 1702.
25. Île Perrot, 1672.
26. Île Bizard, 1678.
27. Île Jésus, 1636.
28. Îles Bourdon, 1672.
29. Île de Montréal, 1640.
30. Île Ste-Thérèse, 1672.
31. Île St-Paul, 1664.
32. Île aux Hérons, 1672.
33. Îles Courcelles, 1673.

Rive Sud:

34. Beauharnois, 1729.
35. Châteauguay, 1673.
36. Îles de la Paix, 1672.
37. Sault-St-Louis, 1680.
38. La Salle, 1750.
39. La Prairie, 1647.
40. Longueuil, 1657, 1698.
41. Du Tremblay, 1672.
42. Boucherville, 1672.
43. Montarville, 1710.

C-8

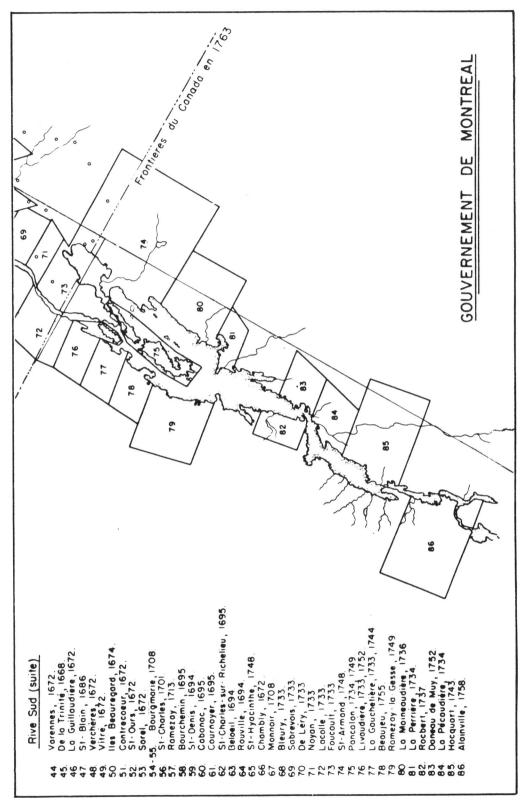

GOUVERNEMENT DE MONTREAL

Frontières du Canada en 1763

Rive Sud (suite)

44. Varennes, 1672.
45. De la Trinité, 1668.
46. La Guilloudière, 1672.
47. St - Blain, 1686.
48. Verchères, 1672.
49. Vitré, 1672.
50. Iles Beauregard, 1674.
51. Contrecoeur, 1672.
52. St-Ours, 1672.
53. Sorel, 1672.
54-55. Bourgmarie, 1708.
56. St-Charles, 1701.
57. Ramezay, 1713.
58. Bourchemin, 1695.
59. St-Denis, 1694.
60. Cabanac, 1695.
61. Cournoyer, 1695.
62. St-Charles- sur- Richelieu, 1695.
63. Beloeil, 1694.
64. Rouville, 1694.
65. St-Hyacinthe, 1748.
66. Chambly, 1672.
67. Monnoir, 1708.
68. Bleury, 1733.
69. Sabrevois, 1733.
70. De Léry, 1733.
71. Noyan, 1733.
72. Lacolle, 1733.
73. Foucault, 1733.
74. St-Armand, 1748.
75. Poncalon, 1734. 1749.
76. Livaudière, 1733, 1752.
77. La Gauchetière, 1733, 1744.
78. Beaujeu, 1755.
79. Ramezay-la-Gesse, 1749.
80. La Moineaudière, 1736.
81. La Perrière, 1734.
82. Rocbert, 1737.
83. Daneau de Muy, 1752.
84. La Pécaudière, 1734.
85. Hocquart, 1743.
86. Alainville, 1758.

C-9

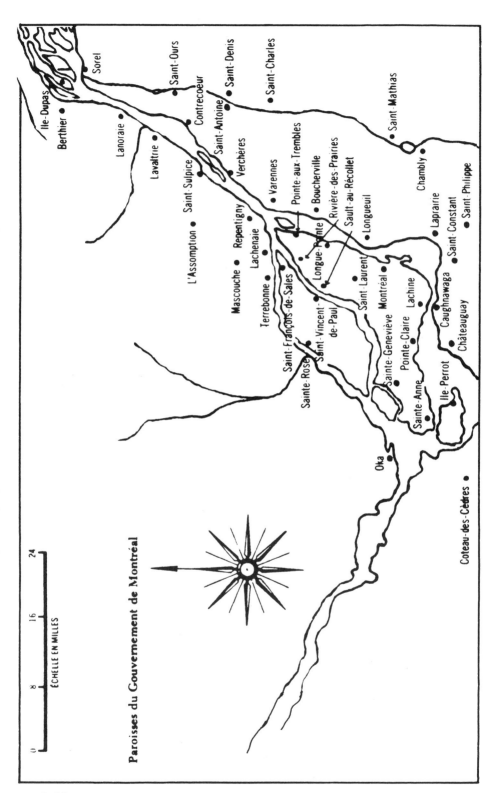

Paroisses du Gouvernement de Montréal

ÉCHELLE EN MILLES

0   8   16   24

C-10

APPENDIX D

The Seigneuries of Beaupre
and the
Ile d'Orleans

The following maps have been reprinted with the gracious permission of LA SOCIETE HISTORIQUE DE QUEBEC. They were taken from the book entitled *Les Seigneuries de Beaupre et de Ile d'Orleans dans leurs debuts,* 1974, by Raymond Gariepy.

The reader of this book is aware by now that most of Our French-Canadian Ancestors settled, at least initially, on land covered by these maps, i.e. Ange-Guardien, Chateau-Richer, Sainte-Anne du Petit-Cap and the Island of Orleans itself.

These land grants were being bought, sold, and exchanged constantly so there is nothing significant about the date 1680. It was selected by the author as a convenient time to fix ownership for historical purposes. This date serves our purpose equally well.

The reader is encouraged to take the time to look up the location of his Ancestors' homestead. It brings a sense of geographic reality to an historical event out of the past.

RIVIÈRE MONTMORENCY

FIEF DE CHARLEVILLE (1677-1694)

2	LOUIS CARREAU dit LA FRAICHEUR
4	FRANÇOIS VÉSINAT
2	LOUIS GARNAULT
3	JEAN GRIGNON
4	CHARLES GARNIER (GERTRUDE COUILLART)
6	RAYMOND PAGET dit QUERCY (CHARLES COUILLART DES ISLETS)
3	JACQUES MARETTE dit LESPINE
3	RENÉ BRISSON
3	JACQUES VÉSINAT
3	PIERRE TESTU DU TILLY
2 2/3	PIERRE MAHEUST des HAZARDS
2 2/3	JEAN TRUDEL
6 2/3	DOMAINE DU FIEF DE CHARLEVILLE
3	THOMAS TOUCHET
3	LAURENT GIGNARD
2	ANTOINE OSSANT
2	JEAN JACQUEREAU
2	JEAN CLEMENT dit LAPOINTE
2	PIERRE BOIVIN
4	NICOLAS QUENTIN dit LA FONTAINE
5	JOSEPH GUION
3	FRANÇOIS HEBERT dit LE COMTE DE ROUSSY
2	CHARLES LETARTRE et MATHURIN HUOT
2	RENÉ LETARTRE
1.7	NICOLAS ROUSSIN
3	Héritiers de DANIEL PERRON dit SUIRE
3	Héritiers de PIERRE GENDREAU dit LA POUSSIERE
3	JACQUES GOULLET
3	ROBERT LABERGE
3.5	DENIS GUION
2.5	CHARLES GODIN
3	NICOLAS ROUSSIN
2	JEAN ROUSSIN
2	GUILLAUME PAGET
4	JEAN MATHIEU

NICOLAS COUILLART DE BELLEROCHE

ARRIERE-FIEF MAQUART (MARGUERITE COUILLART)

8 Arpents de MARG. NICOLET (Fief LEGARDEUR)

7 Arpents de GERMAIN LE BARBIER

ARRIERE-FIEF MAQUART

8 Arpents de LOUIS COUILLART DE LESPINAY

9.7 Arpents de GUILLAUME COUILLART DES CHESNES

12 Arpents d'OLIVIER LETARDIF

GUILLEMETTE HEBERT (ép. G. COUILLART)

MARIE COUILLART (ép. FRANÇOIS BISSOT)

1ère ÉGLISE
2ième ÉGLISE

FIEF DE LOTINVILLE (1652-1690)

2	PIERRE TREMBLAY
1	RENÉ GOULLET
3	ADRIEN HAYOT
2	MICHEL GUION DU ROUVRAY
2	PIERRE TRUDEL
3	ABRAHAM FISET
3	ESTIENNE JACOB
3	THOMAS LEFEBVRE
3	LOUIS LEVASSEUR
6	DOMAINE DU FIEF DE LOTINVILLE

RIV. E. Petit pré

L'ANGE-GARDIEN EN 1680

D-2

Riviere du Petit-Pré

Moulin à farina (1695) — 6 — JULIEN ALLARD

Terres des Legardeur

2	Veuve LOUIS JOBIDON	
2	PIERRE VOYER	
4	ROMAIN TRESPAGNY	
2	LOUIS DESMOULINS	
5.5	CHARLES LE FRANÇOIS	
3	CHARLES BELLENGER	
2	FRANÇOIS GARIÉPY	
2	FRANÇOIS LEFRANC	
2	LOUIS MARTHELOT	
3	CHARLES BELLANGER	
3	BERTRAND CHESNAY DE LA GARENNE	
6	ZACHARIE CLOUTIER FILS	
6	MACE GRAVELLE	
8.8	GUILLAUME BOUCHER	

Riv. Cosault

2.5	Veuve TOUSSAINT TOUPIN du SAULT	
2.5	CHARLES LE TARDIF	
1.5	DOMAINE DE BEAUPRÉ	NICOLAS HUOT
1.5	THOMAS GRANDERIE DIT FAVEROLLE	
6	JACQUES COCHON DIT LA MOTTE	
3.5	SÉMINAIRE DE QUÉBEC (JEAN JOLLIN en 1683)	
3.5	BARTHÉLEMY VERREAU	
6.2	ANTOINE TOUPIN	
6	JEAN CLOUTIER	
6.13 pi	GUILLAUME THIBAULT	
4.13 pi.	CHARLES CLOUTIER	
2	PIERRE MOISAN	
4	JEAN COCHON Fils	
8.8	PIERRE GAGNON	
6	MATHURIN GAGNON	
5	MICHEL ROULLOIS	
3.7	PIERRE et ALEXIS GRAVELLE	
4	Héritiers de JEAN DOYON	
2	JACQUES LE SOT	
2	JACQUES DAVID dit PONTIFÉ	
7	Héritiers de JEAN GAGNON Père	
4	JEAN GAGNON Fils de PIERRE	
2	MARTIN GUÉRARD	
6	ROBERT DROUIN	
12	ESTIENNE RACINE	

Église du CHÂTEAU-RICHER

Moulin à farine

Sault-à-la-Puce

Riviere-aux-Chiens

CHÂTEAU-RICHER en 1680

RIVIÈRE AUX CHIENS

SAINTE-ANNE DU PETIT-CAP EN 1680
ET LES
PREMIÈRES CONCESSIONS ACCORDÉES
PAR LE
SÉMINAIRE DE QUÉBEC A ST-JOACHIM

12	ESTIENNE RACINE	
2.1	NOËL RACINE	
2	FRANÇOIS SAUVIN DIT LA ROSE	
2	JACQUES GAMACHE	
4	JEAN PARÉ	
4	ROBERT PARÉ	
3	NOËL SIMARD	
4	PIERRE SIMARD DIT LOMBRETTE	
4	Héritiers de MATHURIN LE MONNIER	
5	PIERRE BOIVIN	
3	GEORGES PELLETIER	
3	ROBERT FOUBERT DIT LA CROIX	
6	CLAUDE POULLAIN	
2	JACQUES GODIN	
2	PIERRE PETIT	
6	ESTIENNE DE LESSART	
4	ROBERT GIGUIÈRE	
2.5	PIERRE MAUFILS	
2.7	JULIEN MERCIER	
5	ROBERT PARÉ	
5	ANDRÉ BERTHELOT DIT LE LOUTRE	
5	JOSEPH CARON	
5	Héritiers de LOUIS GUIMONT	
3	JOSEPH GUIMONT	
2.7	JEAN BARETTE	
3	RENÉ DE LA VOYE	
3	ANDRÉ BERTHELOT DIT LE LOUTRE	
3.5	JEAN-BAPTISTE CARON	
3.5	JEAN LE PICART	
3	PIERRE GAGNON Fils	
3	SYLVAIN LE VEAU	
5	PIERRE GAGNON Fils	
5	FRANÇOIS LA CROIX	
3	JEAN LE PICART	
2	JEAN BOUTIN DIT LA ROSE	
3	Héritiers de JACQUES DODIER	
3	LAURENT MIGNERON	
3	Héritiers de PIERRE FRICHET	
3	MATHURIN GAGNON Fils	
3	JEAN POULLAIN	

Église de STE-ANNE

à GRANDE RIVIÈRE
ou
Rivière
STE-ANNE

3	NOËL PARÉ	1683
3	LOUIS GASNIER	1683
3	JEAN BOUCHER	1685
3	IGNACE POULLAIN	1686
3	GUILLAUME MOREL	1684
3	CLAUDE GRAVELLE	1684
3	JEAN GRAVELLE	1684
3	ALEXIS GRAVELLE	1684

Riv. Blondel

D-4

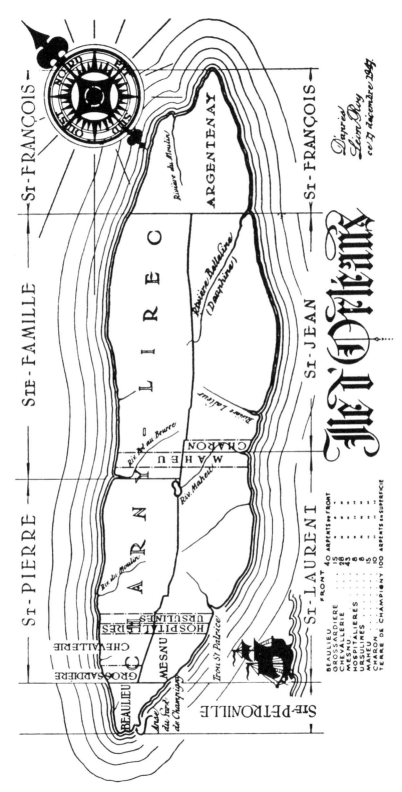

Île d'Orléans

D'après Léon Roy ce 17 décembre 1949.

	FRONT 40 ARPENTS PAR FRONT
BEAULIEU	
GROSSARDIERE	15
CHEVALLERIE	28
MESNU	43
HOSPITALIERES	8
URSULINES	8
MAHEU	15
CHARON	10
TERRE DE CHAMPIGNY 100 ARPENTS en SUPERFICIE	

APPENDIX E

An Index of Names

APPENDIX F

A Comparative Table

THE ANCESTOR	HIS PROVINCE OF ORIGIN	HIS OCCUPATION
1. Nicolas Audet	Poitou	Porter
2. Damien Berube	Normandy	Stonemason
3. Pierre Blais	Angoueme	Farmer
4. Pierre Blanchet	Picardy	Weaver
5. Guillaume Couture	Normandy	Interpreter
6. Gregoire Deblois	Poitou (?)	Prison Guard
7. Antoine Dionne	Unknown	Farmer
8. Julien Fortin	Perche	Butcher
9 a. Jean Gagnon	Perche	Businessman
9 b. Mathurin Gagnon	Perche	Businessman
9 c. Pierre Gagnon	Perche	Businessman
9 d. Robert Gagnon	Perche	Businessman
10. Antoine Lacasse	Anjou	Farmer
11. Francois Lavergne	Limousin	Stonemason
12. Nicolas Leroy	Normandy	Gamewarden
13. Etienne Lessard	Normandy (?)	Boatman
14. Robert Levesque	Normandy	Carpenter
15. Nicolas Paquin	Normandy	Miller
16. Pierre Paradis	Perche	Toolmaker
17. Leonard Pilote	Aunis	Cooper
18. Jean Baptiste Pothier	Orleans	Royal Notary
19. Rene Rheaume	Aunis	Carpenter
20. Pierre Rondeau	Poitou	Farmer
21. Simon Savard	Ile-de-France	Cartwright
22. Etienne Trudeau	Aunis	Carpenter
23. Paul Vachon	Poitou	Estate Notary
24. Nicolas Veilleux	Normandy	Sailor

A Comparative Table

	HIS WIFE	HER PROVINCE OF ORIGIN	THEIR DATE OF MARRIAGE
1.	Magdelaine Despres	Ile-de-France	15 September 1670
2.	Jeanne Sauvenier	Ile-de-France	22 August 1679
3.	Anne Perrot	Ile-de-France	11 October 1668
3.	Elizabeth Royer	Quebec	5 June 1689
4.	Marie Fournier	Quebec	17 February 1670
5.	Anne Esmard	Poitou	18 November 1649
6.	Francoise Viger	Anjou	11 September 1662
7.	Catherine Ivory	Unknown	Unknown
8.	Genevieve Gamache	Ile-de-France	11 November 1652
9 a.	Marguerite Cauchon	Normandy	29 July 1640
9 b.	Francoise Boudeau	Normandy	30 September 1647
9 c.	Vincente Desvarieux	Normandy	14 September 1642
9 d.	Marie Parenteau	Aunis	3 October 1657
10.	Francoise Pitye	Ile-de-France	14 October 1665
11.	Francoise Lefrancois	Normandy	19 October 1671
11.	Jeanne Chartier	Ile-de-France	10 September 1702
11.	Renee Birette	Aunis	15 April 1709
12.	Jeanne Lelievre	Normandy	unknown date, 1657 (?)
13.	Marguerite Sevestre	Quebec	8 April 1652
14.	Jeanne Le Chevalier	Normandy	22 April 1679
15.	Marie Francoise Plante	Quebec	18 November 1676
16.	Barbe Guyon	Normandy	about 1633
17.	Denise Gaultier	Aunis	26 May 1644
18.	Marie-Etiennette Beauvais	Quebec	14 June 1688
19.	Marie Chauvreau	Orleans	29 October 1665
20.	Catherine Verrier	Normandy	30 September 1669
20.	Marie Ancelin	Quebec	5 September 1683
21.	Marie Hourdouille	Ile-de-France	15 June 1644
22.	Adrienne Barbier	Quebec	10 January 1667
23.	Marguerite Langlois	Quebec	22 October 1653
24.	Marguerite Hyardin	Ile-de-France	5 October 1665

(for your convenience)

WIFE   The   FAMILY   HUSBAND

Name		
DOB		
DOM		
D/B		
F		
M		
O		

Remarks

CHILDREN

#	S	Name	DOB	SPOUSE	DOB	DOM
1						
2						
3						

4					
5					
6					
7					
8					
9					
10					
11					
12					
13					
14					

Sources

References & Remarks

KEY

DOB = Date of Birth DOM D/B = Died/Buried F = Father M = Mother O = Other S = Sex

«A défaut de savoir où l'on va,

on peut savoir d'où l'on vient!»